GOLDMINE

For SATBBB a cappella

Duration: ca. 3:50

Arranged by
MERVYN WARREN

Words and Music by
MERVYN WARREN and CLAUDE McKNIGHT

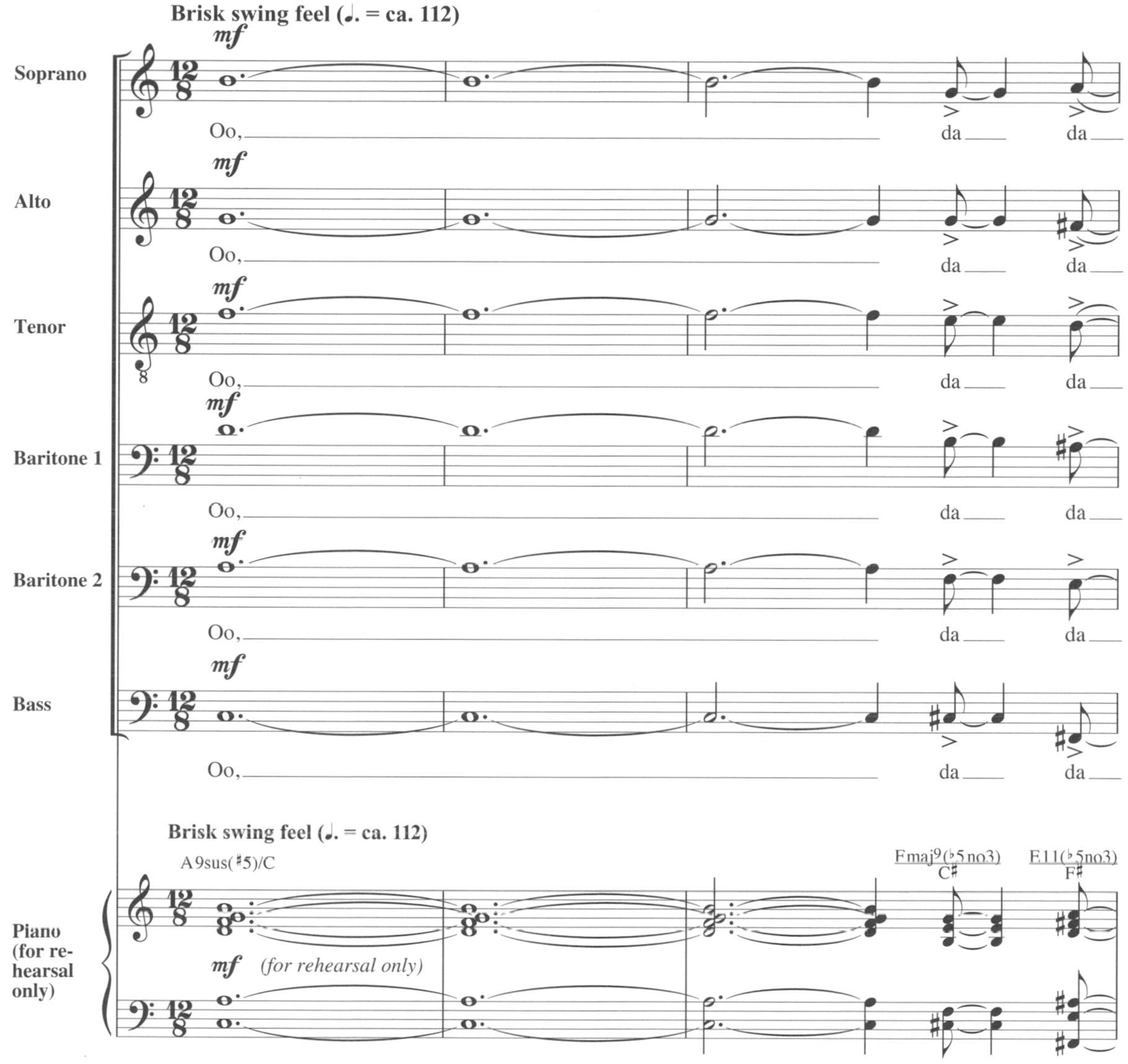

Visit Hal Leonard Online at
www.halleonard.com

ya da da.
Da da da da da da da da
ya da da.
Da da da da da da da da
ya da da.
Da da da da da da da da
da doo doo doo doo doo
da doo doo doo doo doo
da doo doo doo doo doo
C2 / B7(no5)
G7(no5)
B
A
Am / A♭7(no5)
Cmaj7(♯5) / A♭7(no3no5)
A / D♭7(no5)
G / D♭7(no5)
8
da da da da da.
Los - ing my mind,
da da da da da.
Los - ing my mind,
da da da da da da da.
Hoo
da da da da da da.
Hoo
da da da da da.
Hoo
da da da da.
Da hoo ba
Dm / E♭(♭5)
G6
A9sus(no5) / F(no3)
E♭maj7(♭5) / F
Dmaj7(♭5)
8
Dmaj7

climb-ing the walls not e - ven know - ing what it was
8vb
climb-ing the walls not e - ven know - ing what it was
hoo hoo hoo hoo
hoo hoo hoo hoo
hoo hoo hoo hoo
doom hoo ba doom hoo ba doom hoo ba doom hoo ba
A♭7sus(♭5)
Gmaj7(♭5)
9
I had to find won-der-ing if I ev - er would.
8vb
I had to find won-der-ing if I ev - er would.
hoo hoo hoo
hoo hoo hoo
hoo hoo hoo
doom hoo ba doom hoo ba doom hoo ba
12

There had to be some kind of
8vb
There had to be some kind of
hoo hoo hoo hoo
hoo hoo hoo hoo
hoo hoo hoo hoo
doom hoo ba doom hoo ba doom hoo ba doom hoo ba
Amaj7(♭5)
15
some - thing or some-one who might bring out the best in me
8vb
some - thing or some-one who might bring out the best in me
hoo hoo hoo hoo
hoo hoo hoo hoo
hoo hoo hoo hoo
doom hoo ba doom hoo ba doom hoo ba doom hoo ba ba
18

on-ly the Great - est ev - er could.
loco
8vb
on-ly the Great - est ev - er could. You
hoo hoo hoo. You
hoo hoo hoo. You
hoo hoo hoo. You
doom hoo doom doo ee ya doom hoo ba doom hoo ba doom.
B♭maj7(♭5)
21
24
Oo, too won-der-ful to ig - nore.
caught my eye with a glow too won-der-ful to ig - nore.
caught my eye with a glow too won-der-ful to ig - nore.
caught my eye with a glow too won-der-ful to ig - nore.
caught my eye with a glow too won-der-ful to ig - nore.
Then You doom doom doom doom doom doom doom doom doom doom
24
B♭maj7(♭5)/C
Cm7(♭5)/D
G♭maj7(♯5)
Bmaj7(♭5)/D♭
Bmaj7(♭5)/G
Cm6/G♭
24

I took one look
I took one look
I took one look
I took one look
I took one look
doom ba doom bet-ter sight, in Your light, shin-ing down
E♭maj9(♭5)
27
through heav-en's door. I nev-er thought I would
through heav-en's door. I nev-er thought I would
through heav-en's door. I nev-er thought I would
through heav-en's door. I nev-er
through heav-en's door. I nev-er
through heav-en's door. Doom doom doom I doom doom doom doom
Amaj9/B
E♭4(add2)
B7(no3no5)
Amaj9(♭5)
B
G♭13(♯11)
Am11(♭5no3)
F
30

ev - er stum - ble out of dark - ness and prize the view, but
ev - er stum - ble out of dark - ness and prize the view, but
ev - er stum - ble out of dark - ness and prize the view, but
ev - er stum - ble out of dark - ness and prize the view, but
ev - er stum - ble out of dark - ness and prize the view, but
doom doom ba doom stum - ble out of dark - nes and prize the view, but doom ba
Cm11
B♭9sus
B♭6 A♭maj7/B♭ A♭/B Bdim Cm7/B Cm9 E♭2/G
33
this time I found a gold - mine in You, in You.
this time I found a gold - mine in You, in You.
this time I found a gold - mine in You, in You.
this time gold - mine in You, in You.
this time gold - mine in You, in You.
doom doom doom doom doom doom ba doom in You, in You.
A♭maj7/B♭
F♯m11
36

39
This is too much. Hard to be-
This is too much. Hard to be-
8vb
Hoo hoo
Hoo hoo
Hoo hoo
Ba doom hoo ba doom hoo ba doom ba
39
A9sus(add3)/G
A9sus(no5)
F7(no3no5)
39
lieve my life is chang - ing, Lord, but now I've got Your touch.
(8vb)
lieve my life is chang - ing, Lord, but now I've got Your touch.
hoo hoo hoo hoo
hoo hoo hoo hoo
hoo hoo hoo hoo
doom hoo ba doom hoo ba doom hoo ba doom hoo doom ba doom da
42

I got-ta keep pass - ing it a-long.
(8vb)
I got-ta keep pass - ing it a-long. Down
hoo hoo hoo. Down
hoo hoo hoo. Down
hoo hoo hoo. Down
doom hoo hm hm ba doom hoo ba doom hoo ba doom
45
48
Oo. I
in my heart, I
in my heart, I
in my heart, I
in my heart, I
Deep down doom doom doom ba doom doom doom doom ba
48
48

knew there'd be Some - one like You some - day.
knew there'd be Some - one like You some - day.
knew there'd be Some - one like You some - day.
knew there'd be Some - one like You some - day.
knew there'd be Some - one like You some - day.
doom ba oom ba doom doom ba doom doom. On the move,
G♭maj7(♭5)/G
50
Hear me; steer me; just lead the way -
Hear me; steer me; just lead the way -
Hear me; steer me; just lead the way -
Hear me; steer me; just lead the way -
Hear me; steer me; just lead the way -
know-ing You've cho-sen me, just lead the way -
52

- ay. I nev - er thought I would
- ay. I nev - er thought I would
- ay. I nev - er thought I would
- ay. I nev - er
- ay. I nev - er
- ay. I ba doom doom doom doom
G♭
C7(no5)
55
ev - er stum - ble out of dark - ness and prize the view, but
ev - er stum - ble out of dark - ness and prize the view, but
ev - er stum - ble out of dark - ness and prize the view, but
ev - er stum - ble out of dark - ness and prize the view, but
ev - er stum - ble out of dark - ness and prize the view, but
doom doom ba doom stum - ble out of dark - ness and prize the doo ee bop oom ba
57

this time I found a gold - mine in You. I have
this time I found a gold - mine in You. I have
this time I found a gold - mine in You. I have
this time gold - mine in You. I have
this time gold - mine in You. I have
doom doom doom doom doom doom ba doom in You. I have
E2 / B♭7(no5)
60
to ad - mit I nev - er thought I would ev - er chance
to ad - mit I nev - er thought I would ev - er chance
to ad - mit I nev - er thought I would ev - er chance
to ad - mit I nev - er ev - er chance
to ad - mit I nev - er ev - er chance
to ad - mit I ba doom doom doom doom doom doo ee ya doom bop chance
E / G7(no5)
F9(b5no3) / G
F7sus(add2) / C
63

up - on a love I could hold on - to, but
up - on a love I could hold on - to, but
up - on a love I could hold on - to, but
up - on a love I could hold on - to, but
up - on a love I could hold on - to, but
up - on a love I could hold on - to, ba doom ba
66
this time I found a gold - mine
this time I found a gold mine in You.
this time I found a gold - mine in You.
this time gold - mine in You.
this time gold - mine in You.
doom doom doom doom doom doo ee ya doom in You.
B♭9
68

I - (h) found a
I - (h) found a
I - (h) found a
I - (h) found a
I - (h) found a
I looked all a - (ha) - round and fi - nal - ly found a ba
70
trea - sure, but it's true.
trea - sure, but it's true.
trea - sure, no one can meas - ure, but it's true.
trea - sure, no one can meas - ure, but it's true.
trea - sure, but it's true.
trea - sure, doom doom doom doom doom doom doom
Cm(maj7♭5)/A♭
72

I can't be - gin
I can't be - gin
I can't be - gin
I can't be - gin
I can't be - gin
doom ba doom ba doom doom doom. I can't be
74
to cal - cu - late
to cal - cu - late
to cal - cu - late
to cal - cu - late
to cal - cu - late
doom doom doom doom doom doom ba doom ba doom doom
C♯m
E7(no5)
76

79
my wealth and I
my wealth and I
my wealth and I
my wealth and I
my wealth and I
doom doom doom wealth and I ba
F
A♭7 (no5)
Bmaj9/C♯
D2
78
nev - er ev - er stum -
nev - er ev - er stum -
nev - er ev - er stum -
nev - er, nev - er ev - er stum -
nev - er, nev - er thought I would ev - er stum -
doom nev - er ev - er stum -
Cm
F♯7 (no5)
D4
F♯7
C2
F♯7
80

- ble out of dark - ness and prize the view, but this time
- ble out of dark - ness and prize the view, but this time I,
- ble out of dark - ness and prize the view, but this time I found
- ble out of dark - ness and prize the view, but this time I found
- ble out of dark - ness and prize the view, but this time I found,
- ble out of dark - ness and prize the view, but this time I found
D(add2)/B B♭9(♯11no5) G♯m9 A2/F♯m(no3) E9 E/D7 F♯9sus(no5)/D7(no3no5) Bm/F♯7(no5) E♭4/F♯7(no5) Am7
82
I found You and find-ers are keep - ers. I
I found You and find-ers are keep - ers. I
You and find-ers are keep - ers. I
You and find-ers are keep - ers. I
I-(h) found You and find-ers are keep - ers. I
You doo doo dah find-ers are keep - ers. I
Am11 E7(no3)/F♯dim Am/F♯dim Dmaj7(add2)/B
85

nev - er thought I would ev - er chance
nev - er thought I would ev - er chance
nev - er thought I would ev - er chance
nev - er ev - er chance
nev - er ev - er chance
doom doom doom doom doom doom ba doom bop chance
88
upon a love I could hold on - to; I
upon a love I could hold on - to; I
upon a love I could hold on - to; I
upon a love I could hold on - to; I
upon a love I could hold on - to; I
upon a love I could hold on doo ee ba oom ba
90

nev - er thought I would ev - er spot
nev - er thought I would ev - er spot
nev - er thought I would ev - er spot
nev - er ev - er spot
nev - er ev - er spot
doom doom doom doom doom doom ba doom bop spot
92
a ray of hope in the res - i - due. I
a ray of hope in the res - i - due. I
a ray of hope in the res - i - due. I
a ray of hope in the res - i - due. I
a ray of hope in the res - i - due. I
a ray of hope in the res - i - due. I
F♯m
E♭aug
94

nev - er thought I would ev - er find
nev - er thought I would ev - er find
nev - er thought I would ev - er find
nev - er ev - er find
nev - er ev - er find
doom doom doom doom doom doom ba doom doo ee oo find
96
an - oth - er pros - pect to in - ter - view, but
an - oth - er pros - pect to in - ter - view, but
an - oth - er pros - pect to in - ter - view, but
an - oth - er pros - pect to in - ter - view, but
an - oth - er pros - pect to in - ter - view, but
an - oth - er pros - pect to in - ter - view, but
Em
G9(no3,5)
98

this time I found a gold - mine in You.
Gm6
F♯7(no5)
100
I have to ad - mit I nev - er…
C6(♭5)
A♭7(no3,5)
F♯9sus(♭5)
G♯
102

SPREAD LOVE

For SATBBB a cappella

Duration: ca. 3:30

Arranged by
MARK KIBBLE and MERVYN WARREN

Words and Music by MARK KIBBLE,
CLAUDE McKNIGHT and MERVYN WARREN

Visit Hal Leonard Online at
www.halleonard.com

He won't ad-mit it, but it's just a mas - que-rade. He's a mod-
Doo,
Doo,
Doo,
Doo,
Benk, ga-benk, benk, benk, benk, benk.
Doom,
D♭9(no5add6)
3
5
- ern day de-ceiv - er with a case of false - hood fev - er, what a shame.
oo. Doo, doo, bop.
oo. Doo, doo, bop.
oo. Doo, doo, bop.
oo. Doo, doo, bop.
doom, doom, doom, doom, doom. A - yum doom, doom, doom, doom, doom.
5
C9(no5add6)
Gm9
Dm7
5

Alto solo
It's a game. Mmm,
Soprano
Ba-doo, ba-doo. Doo, doo, doo, doo,
Ba-doo, ba-doo. Doo, doo, doo, doo,
Ba-doo, ba-doo. Doo, doo, doo, doo, doo, doo,
Ba-doo, ba-doo. Doo, doo, doo, doo, doo, doo,
Doom, doom, doom, doom, doom, doo, doo. Doo, doo, doo,
C/F
F♯7 (no5)
Dmaj9(♭5 no3)/E
7
9
and then there's dear ole Sis - ter Sa - rah, ain't she sweet?
doo, doo. Oh, yes, she is,
doo, doo. Oh, yes, she is,
doo, doo. Oh, yes, she is,
doo, doo. Oh, yes, she is,
bop, ga-benk, benk, doom, benk, benk, doom, doom, doom. Bow - oom,
9
D7(♯9no5)
C4/D(no5)
D7(♯5)/D
Fmaj7(♭5)/G
9

She gets the word; next thing you know, it's in the street. By the time
yes, doo, doo. Bop.
yes, doo, doo. Bop.
yes, doo, doo. Bop.
yes, doo, doo. Bop.
opt. or additional ad lib.
benk, benk, benk, benk, benk, benk. Doo - up, doo, doo-up, bop. Doom,
Dm9
D♭7(♯11no5)
11
13
s'been re - peat-ed, all the truth has been de - let - ed. A what a shame.
Oo, ba -
Oo, ba -
Oo, ba -
Oo, ba -
doom, doom, doom, doom, doom, a - doom, doom, doom, doom, doom, doom,
13
B♭(add2)/G
13

Hmmph, hmmph, hm-noth - er game.
doo, bop, ba-doo-ee-oo, oo. Dowm, oo.
doo, bop, ba-doo-ee-oo, oo. Oo.
doo, bop, ba-doo-ee-oo, oo. Oo.
doo, bop, ba-doo-ee-oo, oo. Oo.
doo, bop, doom, doom, doom, doom, doom. Bahm, doom, doom, oo.
D7(no5add6)
15
17
Alto solo ends
Soprano
Seems like ev - 'ry-thing you hear is just a tale, but
Ba, doom, ba, doom, doom, doom, doom, ba,
17
F(add4)/C
17

I've got some - thing that will nev - er, ev - er fail. It's called
Dah, dah, dah, dah. Oo, dat. Dah, dah,
Dah, dah, dah, dah. Oo, dat. Dah, dah,
Dah, dah, dah, dah, ba, dup, ba, bup. Dah, dah,
Dah, dah, dah, dah, ba, dup, ba, bup. Dah, dah,
dah, dah, dah, dah, ba, dup, ba, bup, doom,
D♭minMaj7(♭5)/E
19
21
Love. Spread Love, oh, in - stead of spread - ing lies.
Spread Love. Dah, dah, dah, doo, doo,
Spread Love. Dah, dah, dah, doo, doo,
Spread Love. Dah, dah, dah, doo, doo,
Spread Love. Dah, dah, dah, doo, doo,
doom, doom, Spread Love. Doom, doom, doom, doom, doom, doom, doom, bink. Doo - bah, doom,
21
B♭maj7(♭5)/C
E♭7/A
C/D
21

Spread Love, oh, the truth needs no dis - guise. I've
Spread Love, dah, dah, dah. Doo,
Spread Love, dah, dah, dah. Doo,
Spread Love, dah, dah, dah. Doo,
Spread Love, dah, dah, dah. Doo,
doom, doom, Spread Love. Doom, doom, doom, doom, doom, doom, doo, doo, doo, doo, doo, doo,
23
25
Alto (Vocal 2)
of-ten said Love could o-pen an - y door. Oh, but I wish
doo.
doo.
doo.
doo.
doo. Ba, doo, ba, doo, doo, ba, doo, doo, doo, doo, ba, doo, ba, doo,
25
C9sus(no5add6)
G(add4)/A A♭9(♯11no5)
25

end Solo
we had much more; more love is what we need.
More Love is what we need.
doo, doo, doo. More Love is what we need.
A♭/B♭ B♭9(no5) G7sus/E♭
E♭9(add6) E♭13(♯11no5) Am7/D
27
30
Tenor solo (Vocal 3)
Dah, dah, dah, dah. Then there's a fam - i - ly that we'll
Dah, dah, dah, dah, doo,
Dah, dah, dah, dah, benk, benk, benk, bah - yeem, benk,
Dmaj9(♭5)/E
29

Spoken:
just call "the Greens". Huh! A-they have sub-scrip-tions to the gos-
doo, how, bwout 'em oo, whuh, woo,
doo, how, bwout 'em oo, whuh, woo,
doo, how, bwout 'em oo, whuh, woo,
doo, how, bwout 'em oo, whuh, woo,
ah, benk, benk, benk, ba-yump, bank, boomp, bah-benk, boomp, bah, benk, bi-yoomp,
G♭maj7(♯5) E♭m6 Am7/G Fmaj7
31
34
-sip mag-a-zines. With a twist-ed sense of vis-ion, they treat rum-
doo, bop, oo.
doo, bop, oo.
doo, bop, oo.
doo, bop, oo.
Bank, a-bank, bah, doom, doom, doom, doom, doom, doom,
Gm(no5)
Bdim(no3)
34
33

- ors like re - li - gion. A - what a shame.
Bah -
Bah -
Bah -
Bah -
bah, dee - ah - bah - doo, bah, doo - bah, doo - bah, doo - bah,
35
It's the "same - o,
doo, bah - doo, bop. Bah - doo, bee - oo, doo.
doo, bah - doo, bop. Bah - doo, bee - oo, doo.
doo, bah - doo, bop. Bah - doo, bee - oo, doo.
doo, bah - doo, bop. Bah - doo, bee - oo, doo.
doo. Bank, bank - a - bank, bank,
36

38
same - o". We - ee - ell. These days, it seems like ev - 'ry - thing we hear
Doo - ee - oo.
Doo - ee - oo.
Doo - ee - oo.
Doo - ee - oo,
doom, doom, doom, doo. Doo, doo,
D9
38
D♭13(no11no5) C9sus
37
s'just a tale, but I be - lieve in some - thing that will
Ah, dah,
Ah, dah,
Ah, dah,
doo, doo, doo. Ah, dah,
bah-doo-be, doo-ee-oo, doom, doom, doo, doo, ah, dah,
39

42
end Tenor solo
Alto solo
nev - er fa - a - ail. Spread Love, in -
dah - ee - ah, ah, Spread Love.
dah - ee - ah, dah - ah, Spread Love.
dah, dah - ah, Spread Love.
dah, dah - ah, Spread Love.
dah, dah, dah, dum, dum, Spread Love. Doom, doom,
A7(♭5) G9(♭5no3)/A
42
41
stead of spread - ing lies.
Dah, dah, dah, doo, doo,
Dah, dah, dah, doo, doo,
Dah, dah, dah, doo, doo,
Dah, dah, dah, doo, doo,
doom, doom, doom, doom, doom, bink, doo - doo, doom,
43

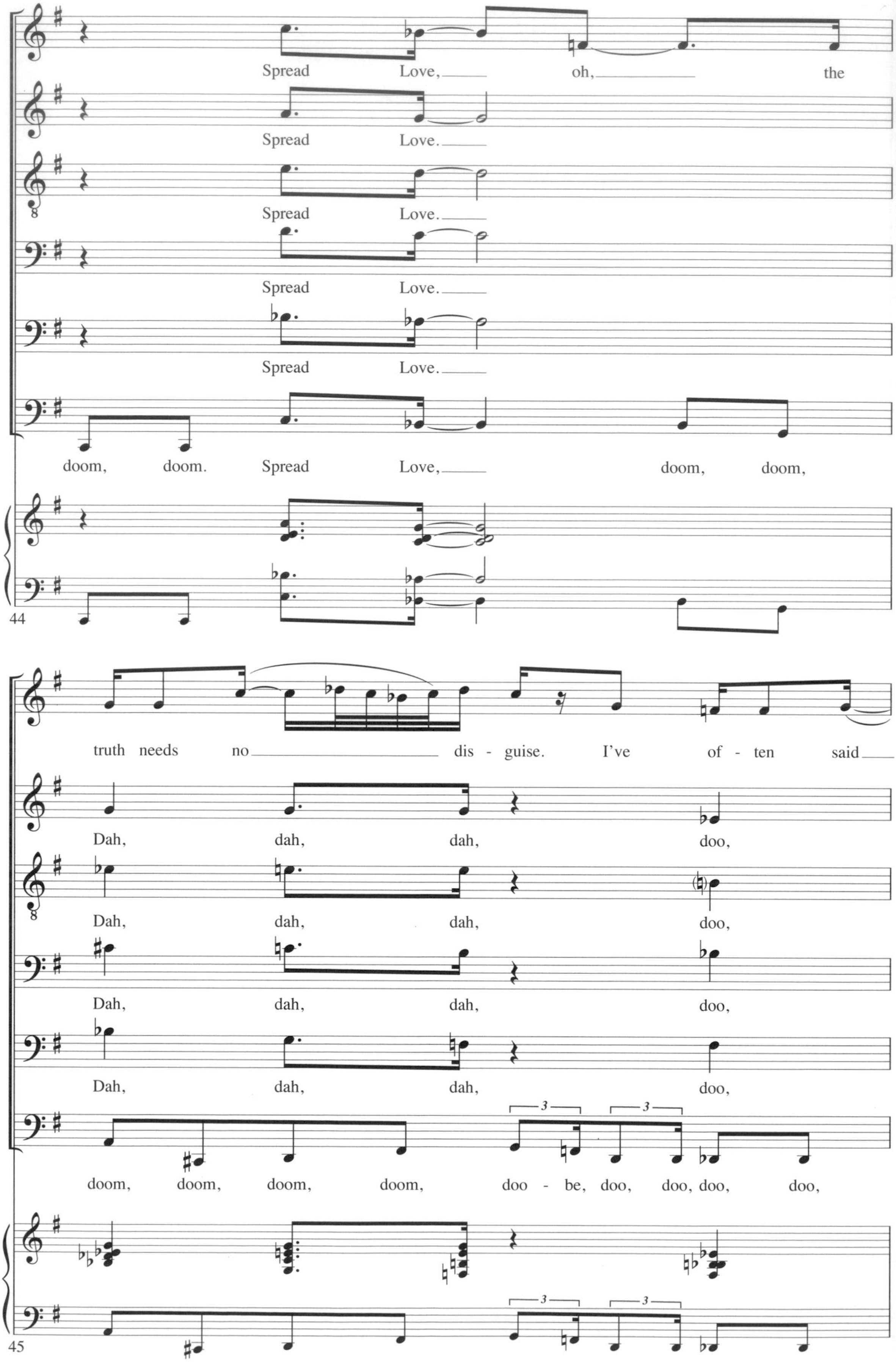
Spread Love, oh, the
Spread Love.
Spread Love.
Spread Love.
Spread Love.
doom, doom. Spread Love, doom, doom,
44
truth needs no dis - guise. I've of - ten said
Dah, dah, dah, doo,
Dah, dah, dah, doo,
Dah, dah, dah, doo,
Dah, dah, dah, doo,
doom, doom, doom, doom, doo - be, doo, doo, doo, doo,
45

46
Love could
doo,
doo,
doo,
doo,
doo, bah - doo - bah - dee - ah, doo - bah - doo,
46
46
Vocal 1
end Alto solo
o-pen an - y door. Oh, but I wish we had much more; more
oo. More
oo. More
oo. More
oo. More
doo, doo, doo, doo - ga, doo - ga, doo, doom, doom, doom, More
47

50
Alto solo (Vocal 2)
Love is what we need. What the world needs now... (I'm tell-in' you;
Love is what we need. What the world needs now
Love is what we need. What the world needs now
Love is what we need. What the world needs now
Love is what we need. What the world needs now
Love is what we need. world needs now
50
B♭2/G(no3)
G♭maj7(♯5)/A♭
49
end Alto solo
Love is what we need.) Love is what we need. What the
is Love; more Love is what we need. What the
is Love; more Love is what we need. What the
is Love; more Love is what we need. What the
is Love; more Love is what we need. What the
is Love; more Love is what we need.
Gm7(no5)
C9(♯11no5)
51

world needs now is Love; more
world needs now is Love; more
world needs now is Love; more
world needs now is Love; more
world needs now is Love; more
world needs now is Love; more
Gm11 A♭13(♯11no5) B♭maj9/C C13(♯11no5)
53
56
Love is what we need. Spread Love
Love is what we need. Spread Love.
Love is what we need. Spread Love.
Love is what we need. Spread Love.
Love is what we need. Spread Love.
Love is what we bah-doo, dum, dum, doom, dum, dum, Spread Love. Doom, doom,
56
55

Vocal 2
'stead of spread - ing lies. Spread Love; the
Dah, dah, dah, doo, doo, Spread Love. Dah,
Dah, dah, dah, doo, doo, Spread Love. Dah,
Dah, dah, dah, doo, doo, Spread Love.
Dah, dah, dah, doo, doo, Spread Love.
doom, doom, doom, doom, doom, bink. Doo-bah, doom, dum, dum, Spread Love. Doom,
57
end Vocal 2
truth needs no dis - guise. I've of - ten
dah, dah, dah. Doo,
dah, dah, dah. Doo,
Dah, dah, dah. Doo,
Dah, dah, dah. Doo,
doom, doom, doom, doom, doom, doom, doom, doom, doom, doom,
59

60
said
Love
could
doom.
Bah - doo - bah, doom,
doom, doom, doom,
60
60
end Vocal 1
Vocal 2
o - pen an - y door. Oh, but I wish we had much more... More
oo. More
oo. More
oo. More
oo. More
doom, doom, doom, bah, doom, ah, doom, doo, doo, doo, More
61

64
Love is what we need, need it. Spread Love
Love is what we need, need it. Spread Love. Hey,
Love is what we need, need it. Spread Love. Hey,
Love is what we need, need it. Spread Love. Hey,
Love is what we need, need it. Spread Love. Hey,
Love is what we need, need it. doom, Spread Love. Doom,doom,
Fmaj9/G
B♭maj7(♭5)/G
64
63
'stead of spread - ing lies. Doo, doo,
dah, dah, dah. Doo, doo,
dah, dah, dah. Doo, doo,
dah, dah, dah. Doo, doo,
dah, dah, dah. Doo, doo,
doom, doom, doom, doom, doom, bink. Doo - bah, doom,
F11sus(♭5)/G
Em7(♭5add4)
65

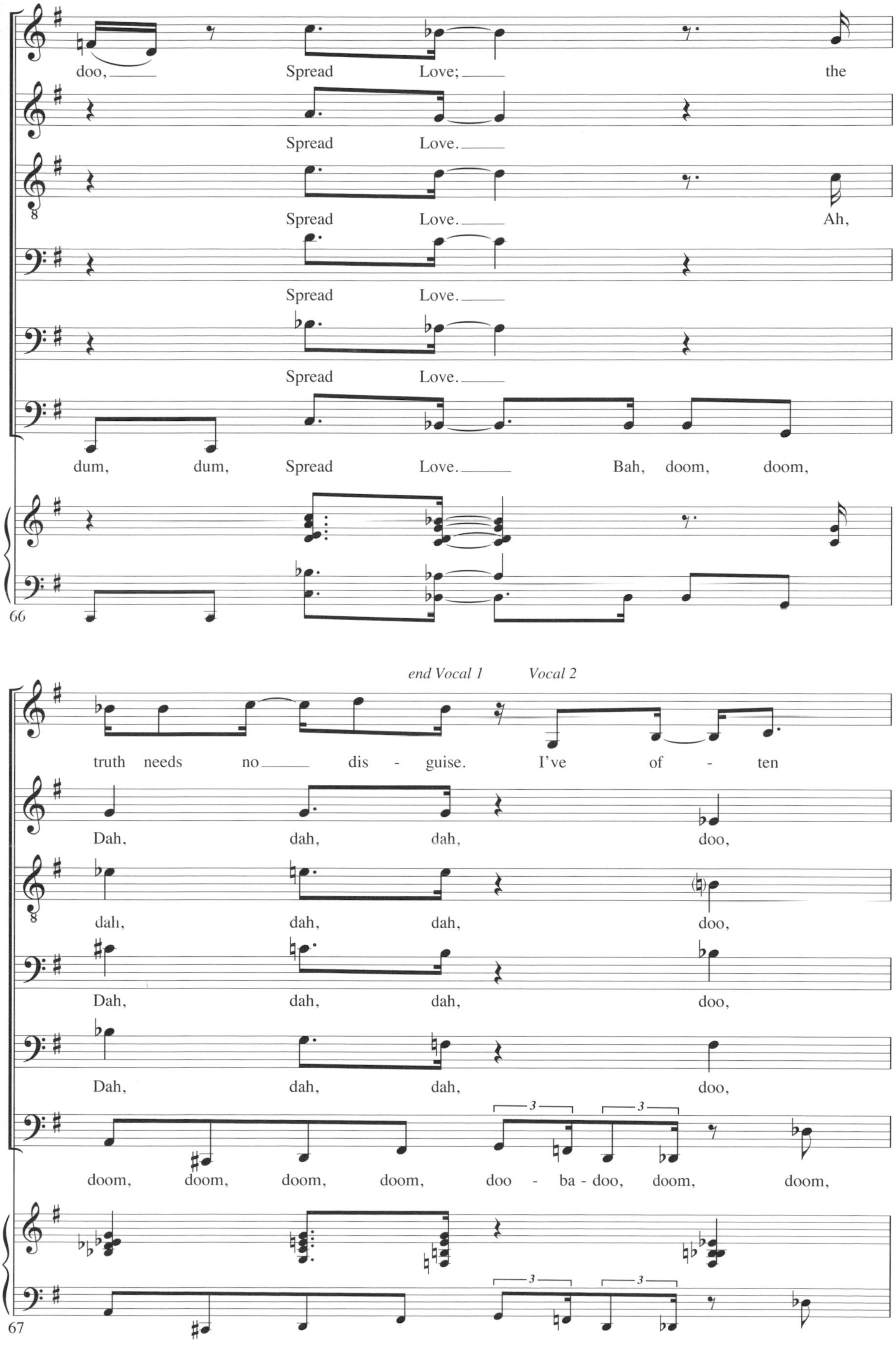
doo, Spread Love; the
Spread Love.
Spread Love. Ah,
Spread Love.
Spread Love.
dum, dum, Spread Love. Bah, doom, doom,
66
end Vocal 1
Vocal 2
truth needs no dis - guise. I've of - ten
Dah, dah, dah, doo,
dah, dah, dah, doo,
Dah, dah, dah, doo,
Dah, dah, dah, doo,
doom, doom, doom, doom, doo - ba - doo, doom, doom,
67

68
end Vocal 2
Vocal 1
said Love could o-pen an - y door, but I wish
doo,
doo,
doo,
doo,
doom, ba-doom, doom, doo, doo, doo. Doo, doo, doo, hmm - mm,
68
68
end Solo
we had much more. Love is what we need, need
oo. More Love is what we need, need
oo. More Love is what we need, need
oo. More Love is what we need, need
oo. More Love is what we need, need
doom, doom, oo, More Love is what we need, need
B♭maj9(no5)
C(no5)
70

72
Spread Love. Dah, dah, dah, doo, doo,
Spread Love. Dah, dah, dah, doo, doo,
Spread Love. Dah, dah, dah, doo, doo,
Spread Love. Dah, dah, dah, doo, doo,
Spread Love. Dah, dah, dah, doo, doo,
72
doom, doom, Spread Love. Doom, doom, doom, doom, doom, doom, doom, bink. Doo-ya-duh,
72
Solo
Spread Love. I've of - ten
Spread Love. Dah, dah, dah, doo,
Spread Love. Dah, dah, dah, doo,
Spread Love. Dah, dah, dah, doo,
Spread Love. Dah, dah, dah, doo,
3
3
dum, dum, Spread Love. Doom, doom, doom, doom, doom, doom, yoo-ba-doo, dum. Dum,
3
3
74

76
said Love could o - pen an - y door, but I wish we had
doom, ba, doom, ba doom, hmm - mm, doom, doom, doo - om, ah-doom, doom,
76
76
end Solo
much more; more Love is what we need.
oo, more Love is what we need.
oo, more Love is what we need.
oo, more Love is what we need.
oo, more Love is what we need.
Spoken:
doom, doom, doom, more Love is what we need. Bank, bank.
78

IF WE EVER NEEDED THE LORD BEFORE (WE SURE DO NEED HIM NOW)

For SATBBB a cappella

Duration: ca. 5:00

Arranged by
MERVYN WARREN

Words and Music by
THOMAS A. DORSEY

sure do need Him now. O Lord, we sure do need Him now,
sure do need Him now. Oh, we sure do need Him now,
sure do need Him now. Oh, we sure do need Him now,
sure do need Him now. Oh, we sure do need Him
sure do need Him now. Oh, we sure do need Him
sure do need Him now. Oh, we sure do need Him
A♭/E♭ B♭13(♯11) D♭maj7/E♭ E♭7
B♭7sus(♯5♯9)
A♭maj7(add2)/F A♭maj9/B♭
Caug7(add2)/B♭ E9
3
O Lord, we sure do need Him now. If we
O Lord, we sure do need Him now. If we
O Lord, we sure do need Him now. If we
now, O Lord, we sure do need Him now. we
now, O Lord, we sure do need Him now. we
now, O Lord, we sure do need Him now. Oh, glo - ry, if we
E♭9 Gmaj7(♭5)/A
F♯9sus(♭5)/D C♯m9
F♯9sus
D♭
E♭(no3)
B♭2 A♭2/F
6

9
ev - er a-need-ed the Lord be-fore, we sure do need Him now.
ev - er a-need-ed the Lord be-fore, we sure do need Him now.
ev - er a-need-ed the Lord be-fore, we sure do need Him now.
ev - er a-need-ed the Lord be-fore, we sure do need Him now.
ev - er a-need-ed the Lord be-fore, we sure do need Him now.
ev - er a-need-ed the Lord be-fore, we sure do need Him now.
9
G♭maj9(♭5)/A♭ G♭maj7(♭5)/A♭ B♭m9 B♭dim7 A♭/C B♭7sus(♭5)/C D♭maj9 E(♯5)/D♭6sus(no5) G♭/C7(no5) B♭4/F
We need Him ev - 'ry day and ev - 'ry
We need Him ev - 'ry day and ev - 'ry
We need Him ev - 'ry day and ev - 'ry
We need Him ev - 'ry day and ev - 'ry
We need Him ev - 'ry day and ev - 'ry
We need Him ev - 'ry day and ev - 'ry
G♭maj9/A♭ B♭sus9/D♭ Cm/D♭6(no5) C♯m9 B♭m7(♭5)/D♭ B♭7 D♭6/E♭ E♭7
12

17
hour. If we ev - er a - need - ed the
hour. ev - er a - need - ed the
hour. ev - er a - need - ed the
hour. ev - er a - need - ed the
hour. ev - er a - need - ed the
hour. ev - er a - need - ed the
D♭4 / F7(no5)
E♭4 / F7(no5)
B / F7(no5)
B/E
E♭4/E
D♭4/E
17
15
Lord be - fore, we sure do need Him now. O Lord, we
Lord be - fore, we sure do need Him now. Oh, we
Lord be - fore, we sure do need Him now. Oh, we
Lord be - fore, we sure do need Him now. Oh, we
Lord be - fore, we sure do need Him now. Oh, we
Lord be - fore, you we we sure do need Him now. Oh, we
18

sure do need Him now. O Lord, we
sure do need Him now. O Lord, we
sure do need Him now. O Lord, we
sure do need Him now. O Lord, we
sure do need Him now. O Lord, we
sure do need Him now. O Lord, we
A13(♯11)
21
sure do need Him now. If we
sure do need Him now. If we
sure do need Him now. If we
sure do need Him now. we
sure do need Him now. we
sure do need Him now. Oh, glo - ry, if - a we
23

25
ever a-needed the Lord before, we
D♭2
E♭m(no5) E♭m9(add4) A♭7/E♭ G♭maj7/A♭
25
sure do need Him now. We need Him ev'ry
27

Solo
day and ev - 'ry hour. We
day and ev - 'ry hour.
day and ev - 'ry hour.
day and ev - 'ry hour.
day and ev - 'ry hour.
day and ev - 'ry hour.
30
33
need Him in the morn - ing.
need Him, need Him, need Him,
need Him, need Him, need Him,
need Him, need Him, need Him,
need Him, need Him, need Him,
need Him, you know that we need, bah - doom, doom, need Him, you know that we
33
33

We need Him in the
need Him, need Him, need Him,
need Him, need Him, need Him,
need Him, need Him, need Him,
need Him, need Him, need Him,
need Him, need Him, a - need Him,
Emaj7/F♯
36
41
night. We need
need Him, need Him, need Him,
need Him, need Him, need Him,
need Him, need Him, need Him,
need Him, need Him, need Him,
need Him, need Him, bah-doom, doom, doom, doom, doom,
G7sus(♭5)/E♭
41 E♭m9(no5add4)
39

Him in the noon - day when the
need Him, need Him, need Him, when the
need Him, need Him, need Him, when the
need Him, need Him, need Him, when the
need Him, need Him, need Him, when the
doom, doom, doom, doom, doom, doom, doom, bah-doom, boom, bah-doom, doom, when the
F7sus/D♭
Emaj7(♯5)/F♯
E6(♭5)
42
end Solo
47
sun is shin - ing bright. If we ev - er a-need - ed the
sun is shin ing bright. If we ev - er a-need - ed the
sun is shin - ing bright. If we ev - er a-need - ed the
sun is shin - ing bright. If we ev - er a-need - ed the
sun is shin - ing bright. If we ev - er a-need - ed the
sun is shin - ing b(a)-right. Oh, glo - ry. If we ev - er a-need - ed the
A♭maj7/E♭ Fm7/E♭
E♭9
47
45

Lord be-fore, we sure do need Him now. Oh, we
Lord be-fore, we sure do need Him now. Oh, we
Lord be-fore, we sure do need Him now. Oh, we
Lord be-fore, we sure do need Him now. Oh, we
Lord be-fore, we sure do need Him now. Oh, we
Lord be-fore, you know, we sure do need Him now. Oh, we
48
sure do need Him now. O Lord, we sure do need Him now.
sure do need Him now. O Lord, we sure do need Him now.
sure do need Him now. O Lord, we sure do need Him now.
sure do need Him now. O Lord, we sure do need Him now.
sure do need Him now. O Lord, we sure do need Him now.
sure do need Him now. O Lord, we sure do need Him now.
51

55
If we ev - er a-need-ed the Lord be-fore, we
If we ev - er a-need-ed the Lord be-fore, we
If we ev - er a-need-ed the Lord be-fore, we
If ev - er a-need-ed the Lord be-fore, we
ev - er a-need-ed the Lord be-fore, we
Oh, glo - ry. If - a we ev - er a-need-ed the Lord be-fore, we
55
54
sure do need Him now. We need Him ev - 'ry
sure do need Him now. We need Him ev - 'ry
sure do need Him now. We need Him ev - 'ry
sure do need Him now. We need Him ev - 'ry
sure do need Him now. We need Him ev - 'ry
sure do need Him now. We need Him ev - 'ry
57

Solo
day and ev - 'ry hour.
We
day and ev - 'ry hour.
day and ev - 'ry hour.
day and ev - 'ry hour.
day and ev - 'ry hour.
day and ev - 'ry hour.
60
63
need Him when we're hap - py.
need Him, need Him, need Him,
need Him, need Him, need Him,
need Him, need Him, need Him,
need Him, need Him, need Him,
need Him, ba doom ma need bah - doom, need Him, bah - doom,
63
63

Ah. We need Him when we're
need Him, need Him, need Him,
need Him, need Him, need Him,
need Him, need Him, need Him,
need Him, need Him, need Him,
doom, moh, need bah-doom, need Him,
66
71
sad. We need
need Him, need Him, need Him,
need Him, need Him, need Him,
need Him, need Him, need Him, whoa,
need Him, oh, need Him, need Him,
need bah-doom, doom, doom, doom, doom, doom, doom, doom, doom, doom, doom,
71
69

Him when we're bur - dened.
need Him, need Him,
need Him, need Him,
need Him, need Him,
need Him, need Him,
doom, doom, doom, doom, doom, doom, doom, doom, doom, bah -
A13(♯11)
72
end Solo
need Him, just to make our hearts fa-heel glad.
need Him, just to make our hearts fa-heel glad.
need Him, just to make our hearts feel glad.
need Him, just to make our hearts feel...
doo we bah doom, bah-doom, just to make our hearts fa-heel oh, glo - ry, a-we
E9sus F♯4(add3)/E
74

77
Him, Him, we real - ly, real - ly, real - ly need Him
Him, Him, we real - ly, real - ly, real - ly need Him
Him, Him, we real - ly, real - ly, real - ly need Him
Him, Him, we real - ly, real - ly, real - ly need Him
Him, Him, we real - ly, real - ly, real - ly need Him
need. we need Him, bah - doom, doom, doom, doom,
77
B7sus(♭5)/C♯ F♯m7 B♭7/F Fm7(add4)/F Em7 E13(no5) Gm11(♭5no3)/A
77
in the morn - ing, in the night.
in the morn - ing, in the night.
in the morn - ing, in the night.
in the morn - ing, in the night.
in the morn - ing, in the night.
doom, in the morn - ing, in the night, we
Cmaj9/D Cmaj9(no5)/D(no5)
79

Solo
We need Him in the noon - day.
Oo, oo, when the
Oo, oo, when the
Oo, oo, when the
Oo, oo, when the
need, bah-doom, dah, dah, dah, dah, dah, when the
F2(add4)/A
81
end Solo
85
Yea - ee-ah, yeah. Oh, Him, Him, we
sun is shin - ing. Oh, Him, Him, we
sun is shin - ing. Oh, Him, Him, we
sun is shin - ing. Oh, Him, Him, we
sun is shin - ing. Oh, Him, Him, we
(lean in)
sun is shin - ing, shin - ing bright. We need. We need. Bah -
F9(♯11no5)
Gm6/G♯
85
83

real - ly need Him when we're hap - py, when we're sad.
real - ly need Him when we're hap - py, when we're sad.
real - ly need Him when we're hap - py, when we're sad.
real - ly need Him when we're hap - py, when we're sad.
real - ly need Him when we're hap - py, when we're sad.
doom, doom, doom, doom, doom, when we're hap - py, when we're sad. Bah-
Em/F♯7 (no5) G/F7 (no5) C/E7 (no5)
86
Oo, oo, oo. jus to make our hearts feel
Oo, oo, oo, jus to make our hearts feel
Oo, oo, oo, jus to make our hearts feel
Oo, oo, oo, jus to make our hearts feel
Solo
end Solo
We need Him when we're bur - dened jus to make our hearts feel
doom, bah - doom, bah-doom, bah-doom, jus to make our hearts feel…
89

93
glad. Him, Him, we
glad. Him, Him, we
glad. Him, Him, we
glad. Him, Him, we
glad. Him, Him, we
Oh, glo - ry, we need, oh, we need. Bah -
92
really, really, really need Him in the morn - ing,
real - ly, real - ly, real - ly, doo, doo, doo, doo, in the morn - ing,
doom, doom, doom, doom, doom, in the morn - ing,
94

Solo
in the night.
We need Him in the noon -
in the night.
Oo, oo,
in the night.
Oo, oo,
in the night.
Oo, oo,
in the night.
Oo, oo,
in thc night.
Bah doom, bah - doo, dah, dah,
96
end Solo
- day.
shin - ing.
Oh, oh,
when the sun is shin - ing,
Oh, oh,
when the sun is shin - ing,
Oh, oh,
when the sun is shin - ing,
Oh, oh,
when the sun is shin - ing,
Oh, oh,
dah, dah, dah, when the sun is shin - ing, shin - ing bright. Oh, we
D9sus(no5)/A Dmaj9(no5)/G♯
98

101
Him, Him, we real - ly need Him
Him, Him, we real - ly need Him
Him, Him, we real - ly need Him
Him, Him, we real - ly need Him
Him, Him, we real - ly need Him
need, we need, bah - doom, doom, doom, doom,
Gm/Csus7
A6 9/F7(no3no5)
A/E♭9(no5)
101
when we're hap - py, when we're sad.
when we're hap - py, when we're sad.
when we're hap - py, when we're sad.
when we're hap - py, when we're sad.
when we're hap - py, when we're sad.
dum, when we're hap - py, when we're sad. Bah -
103

Oo, oo, oo, jus to
Oo, oo, oo, jus to
Oo, oo, oo, jus to
Oo, oo, oo, jus to
Solo
We need Him when we're bur - dened jus to
end Solo
doom, bah - doom, bah - doom, bah - doom, jus to
105
109
make our hearts feel… If we ev - er a - need - ed the
make our hearts feel… If we ev - er a - need - ed the
make our hearts feel… If we ev - er a - need - ed the
make our hearts feel… If we ev - er a - need - ed the
make our hearts feel… If we ev - er a - need - ed the
make our hearts feel… ev - er a - need - ed the
109
107

Lord be-fore, we sure do need Him now. O Lord, we
Lord be-fore, we sure do need Him now. Oh, we
Lord be-fore, we sure do need Him now. Oh, we
Lord be-fore, we sure do need Him now. Oh, we
Lord be-fore, we sure do need Him now. Oh, we
Lord be-fore, I know we sure do need Him now. Oh, we
110
sure do need Him now, O Lord, we
sure do need Him now, O Lord, we
sure do need Him now, O Lord, we
sure do need Him now, O Lord, we
tr
sure do need Him now, O Lord, we
tr
sure do need Him now, O Lord, we
G9sus(no5)/E♭
113

sure do need Him now. If we
sure do need Him now. If we
sure do need Him now. If we
sure do need Him now. If we
sure do need Him now.
sure do need Him now. Oh, glo - ry. If we
F♯m(add2) F♯4(add2)
115
117
ev - er a - need - ed the Lord be - fore, we sure
ev - er a - need - ed the Lord be - fore, we sure
ev - er a - need - ed the Lord be - fore, we sure
ev - er a - need - ed the Lord be - fore, we sure
ev - er a - need - ed the Lord be - fore, we sure
ev - er a - need - ed the Lord be - fore, we sure
117
Gmaj9(add6no3)/E
E(no3)
D♭7(♯5)
B4
D♭aug
D♭4
D2
117

do need Him now. We need Him ev - 'ry
B4(add6)/F♯(no3)
D♭4(add6)/E
119
day and ev - 'ry hour.
day and ev - 'ry… Doo, doo,
day and ev - 'ry, bah - doom, bah - doom, bah-
D/E
122

126
We need Him ev - 'ry day
doo, doo, need Him ev - 'ry day
doo, doo, need Him ev - 'ry day
doo, doo, need Him ev - 'ry day
doo, doo, need Him ev - 'ry day
doom, bah-doom, we need Him ev - 'ry day
126
125
and ev - 'ry hour. We
and ev - 'ry... Doo, doo, doo, doo,
and ev - 'ry... Doo, doo, doo, doo,
and ev - 'ry... Doo, doo, doo, doo,
and ev - 'ry... Doo, doo, doo, doo,
and ev - 'ry, bah - doom, bah-doom, bah - down, bah-doom, we
128

need Him ev - 'ry day and ev - 'ry
need Him ev - 'ry day and ev - 'ry…
need Him ev - 'ry day and ev - 'ry…
need Him ev - 'ry day and ev - 'ry…
need Him ev - 'ry day and ev - 'ry…
need Him ev - 'ry day and ev - 'ry, bah-
131
136
hour. Min-ute, by min-ute, by min-ute, we need Him ev - 'ry
Doo, doo, doo, doo, need Him ev - 'ry
Doo, doo, doo, doo, need Him ev - 'ry
Doo, doo, doo, doo, need Him ev - 'ry
Doo, doo, doo, doo, need Him ev - 'ry
doom, bah-doom, bah-doom, bah-doom, bah-doom, we need Him ev - 'ry
136
134

day and ev - 'ry hou -
day, 'ry
day, ev - 'ry
day, ev - 'ry
day, ev - 'ry
day a ay bah-doom, bah-doom, bah-
Am11(♭5no3)/F
Em7
137
- ur.
day and, and ev - 'ry hour.
day and, and ev - 'ry hour.
day and, and ev - 'ry hour.
day and, and ev - 'ry hour.
doom, bah-doom, bah-doom, and ev - 'ry hour.
F7/B
140

A QUIET PLACE

For SATBBB a cappella

Duration: ca. 2:45

Words and Music by
RALPH CARMICHAEL

Visit Hal Leonard Online at
www.halleonard.com

rap - id pace where God can soothe my
rap - id pace where God can soothe my
rap - id pace God can soothe my
rap - id pace God can soothe my
rap - id pace God can soothe my
rap - id pace God can soothe my
G♯4/A Am7 C(♭5)/G♯ A6/9 Gaug(no5) E9sus/G A6/9 Gaug(no3) F♯m7
4
9
trou - bled mind. Shel - tered by
trou - bled mind. Shel - tered by
trou - bled mind. Shel - tered by
trou - bled mind. Shel - tered by
trou - bled mind. Shel - tered by
trou - bled mind. Shel - tered by
9
F♯4/G♯ G♯m7(♭5) Gmaj7/A Gmaj9(♭5)/A Cmaj9(add2)/A Am7(♭13 ♯11)
7

tree and flow'r, there, in my qui - et hour with
Cmaj9/D D9sus D7(no3)/F♯7(no5) D2/F♯7(no5) B7sus/G(no3) Em11 Em9 C13(♯11)
10
Him, my cares are
Bm9 B/A Bmaj9/G♯ G/C♯7(no5)
13

17
left be - hind. Wheth - er a
left be - hind. Oo,
left be - hind. Oo,
left be - hind. Oo,
left be - hind. Oo,
left be - hind. Oo,
D♭6(no3)/C♯ G♭/D♭ B♭m/D♭
B7(no5)/A7(no5)
C(add2)/A F♯7sus/A
15
gar - den small, or on a
oo,
oo,
oo,
oo,
oo,
C♯m7(♭5)
C/F♯ C♯m/F♯ Asus/F♯
B♭maj7sus(no5)/F♯7(no5no3)
18

moun - tain tall, new strength and cour - age
oo, new strength and cour - age
A♭9(♯11no5)
Gmaj9
F♯9sus
F♯7(♭9)
20
25
there I find. Then from this
Am11(no5)
D13(no11)/A
B♭aug(add2)/G6(no3no5)
23

qui - et place, I go pre - pared to face a
qui - et place, I go pre - pared to face
E9sus(♭5) Gm6/F♯ Amaj9/B A/B Amaj7/B B9(no5,add6) B9
26
new day with love for all man - kind. Oo,
new day with love for all man - kind. Oo,
G2/Em(no3) G/A G(♭5)/A Gdim7/A F6(no3)/B♭ C(add2)/B♭
29

oo.
oo.
oo.
oo.
oo.
oo.
F13(♯11) G7sus(♭5)/E♭ Dm9(no5,add4)
F9sus(no5) E♭maj7(no3)/F F13(♯11,no9)
32
Wah, wah.
Wah, oh.
Wah, oh.
Wah, oh.
Wah, oh.
Wah, oh.
B♭maj9 G9sus/E♭ C9sus/E♭ Gm/A Em7(♭5)/A A7
A♭6(no3)/A♭ D♭/A♭ A♭6/A♭ D♭6/A♭
35

Then from this
Then, oo,
Then, oo,
Then, oo,
Then, oo,
Then, oo,
D♭7/G
G♭maj9
38
40
qui - et place, I go pre - pared to face a
oo,
oo,
oo,
oo,
oo,
40
Fdim/B7(no5)
D♭(add2)/B7(no3no5)
40

new day with love for all man -
with love for all man -
B
E♭7 (no5)
43
kind.
kind, for all man - kind.
rit.
Em
C♯7 (no5)
Bm
F♯m
E²
E
46

MARY

For SATBBB a cappella

Duration: ca. 3:30

Arranged by
MARK KIBBLE

Traditional

Visit Hal Leonard Online at
www.halleonard.com

- ry.
Tell Mar - tha not to mourn.
Oh, Ma - ry, don't you weep.
Oh, Ma - ry, don't you weep.
Oh, Ma - ry, don't you weep.
Oh, Ma - ry, don't you weep.
Oh, Ma - ry, don't you weep. Bom, bom, bom, bom, bom, bom, bom,
B♭
3
Well, well, well,
Mar - tha, don't you mourn.
Mar - tha, don't you mourn.
Mar - tha, don't you mourn.
Mar - tha, don't you mourn.
bom. Mar - tha, don't you mourn.
E♭/B♭ D♭/B♭ E♭/C D♭
5

Ma - ry. Tell Mar - tha not
Oh, oh, Ma - ry, don't you weep.
Oh, oh, Ma - ry, don't you weep.
Oh, oh, Ma - ry, don't you weep.
Oh, oh, Ma - ry, don't you weep.
Oh, oh, Ma - ry, don't you weep. Bom, bom, bom, bom, bom, bom, bom,
E♭9
D♭maj7/B♭
7
to mourn 'cause Pha - roah's ar -
Mar - tha, don't you mo, oh, oh,
Mar - tha, don't you mo, oh, oh,
Mar - tha, don't you mo, oh, oh,
Mar - tha, don't you mo, oh, oh,
bom. Mar - tha, don't you mo, oh, oh,
Gsus(♭5)/B♭
A♭
A
9

my.
Don - cha know dey been drowned?
ourn, Pha - roah's ar - my
D♭/F Cm7/F D♭
E♭ D♭/E♭ Cm/E♭
11
Lawd,
a - sing - in', Ma -
drowned in the Red Sea.
B♭m7 E♭/D♭ D♭/D
D♭maj7/E♭
13

- ry. Tell Mar - tha not to
Oh, Ma - ry, don't you weep.
Oh, Ma - ry, don't you weep.
Oh, Ma - ry, don't you weep.
Oh, Ma - ry, don't you weep.
Oh, Ma - ry, don't you weep.
A♭maj6/B♭
15
mourn, Well, well, sing - in',
Mar - tha, not to mo, oh, oh,
Mar - tha, not to mo, oh, oh,
Mar - tha, not to mo, oh, oh,
Mar - tha, not to mo, oh, oh,
Mar - tha, not to mo, oh, oh,
Gdim/B♭
17

19
Ma - ry.
Tell Mar - tha not to
ourn, oh, Ma - ry, don't you weep.
ourn, oh, Ma - ry, don't you weep.
ourn, oh, Ma - ry, don't you weep.
ourn, oh, Ma - ry, don't you weep.
ourn, oh, Ma - ry, don't you weep. Bom, bom, bom, bom, bom, bom, bom,
19
19
mourn.
Well, well, well, well, well,
Mar - tha, don't you mo -
Mar - tha, don't you mo -
Mar - tha, don't you mo -
Mar - tha, don't you mo -
bom. Mar - tha, don't you mo -
21

Ma - ry, yeah. Tell Mar - tha not to
ourn, no, Ma - ry, don't you weep.
ourn, no, Ma - ry, don't you weep.
ourn, no, Ma - ry, don't you weep.
ourn, no, Ma - ry, don't you weep.
ourn, no, Ma - ry, don't you weep. Bom, bom, bom, bom, bom, bom, bom,
Fm7/B♭
23
mourn 'cause Pha - roah's ar -
Mar - tha, don't you mourn. Oh, oh,
Mar - tha, don't you mourn. Oh, oh,
Mar - tha, don't you mourn. Oh, oh,
Mar - tha, don't you mourn. Oh, oh,
bom. Mar - tha, don't you mourn. Oh, oh,
25

27
my.
Don - cha know dey been drowned?
oh, Pha - roah's ar - my
oh, Pha - roah's ar - my
oh, Pha - roah's ar - my
oh, Pha - roah's ar - my
oh, Pha - roah's ar - my
27
27
Sing - in', Ma -
drowned in the Red Sea,
drowned in the Red Sea,
drowned in the Red Sea,
drowned in the Red Sea,
drowned in the Red Sea,
29

ry.
Tell Mar - tha not
Oh, Ma - ry, don't you weep.
31
to mourn.
I'm sing - in', Ma -
Mar - tha, not to mo oh, oh,
33

35
ry. I be - lieve that I
ourn, if I could,
ourn, if I could,
ourn, if I could,
ourn, if I could,
ourn, if I could,
35
35
would. Well, would I put my foot on
I sure - ly would
I sure - ly would
I sure - ly would
I sure - ly would
I sure - ly would
A♭7/D B♭9 Fm11(no5) E9(no5♯11)
37

3
that rock where Mo - ses stood?
stand on the rock.
stand on the rock.
stand on the rock.
stand on the rock.
(ad lib. fill)
stand on the rock. Doom, doom,
E♭9sus
39
'Cause Pha - roah's ar -
Mo - ses stood. Oh, oh,
Mo - ses stood. Oh, oh,
Mo - ses stood. Oh, oh,
Mo - ses stood. Oh, oh,
doom, Mo - ses stood. Oh, oh,
41

- my, don - cha know, dey been drowned?
oh, Pha - roah's ar - my
oh, Pha - roah's ar - my
oh, Pha - roah's ar - my
oh, Pha - roah's ar - my
43
oh, Pha - roah's ar - my
43
Sing - in', Ma -
drowned in the Red Sea.
drowned in the Red Sea.
drowned in the Red Sea.
drowned in the Red Sea.
drowned in the Red Sea.
45

- ry. Tell Mar - tha not to
Oh, Ma - ry, don't you weep.
Oh, Ma - ry, don't you weep.
Oh, Ma - ry, don't you weep.
Oh, Ma - ry, don't you weep.
Oh, Ma - ry, don't you weep.
47
mourn. One more time sing - in',
Mar - tha, don't you mourn. Oh, oh,
Mar - tha, don't you mourn. Oh, oh,
Mar - tha, don't you mourn. Oh, oh,
Mar - tha, don't you mourn. Oh, oh,
Mar - tha, don't you mourn. Oh, oh,
49

51
Ma - ry.
I, I, I,
oh, if I could,
oh, if I could,
oh, if I could,
oh, if I could,
oh, if I could, a - doom, doom, a - doom,
51
I,
I'm gon-na stand
I sure - ly would
I sure - ly would
I sure - ly would
I sure - ly would
doom, I sure - ly would
A♭7/C
53

on the rock where Mo - ses stood. 'Cause Pha - roah's ar -
stand on the rock where Mo - ses stood. Oh, oh,
stand on the rock where Mo - ses stood. Oh, oh,
stand on the rock where Mo - ses stood. Oh, oh,
stand on the rock where Mo - ses stood. Oh, oh,
stand on the rock duhm, doom, doom, Mo - ses stood. Oh, oh,
3
55
57

59
- my,
don - cha know, they got drowned?
oh, Pha - roah's ar - my
oh, Pha - roah's ar - my
oh, Pha - roah's ar - my
oh, Pha - roah's ar - my
oh, Pha - roah's ar - my
59
59
Sing - in', Ma -
drowned in the Red Sea.
drowned in the Red Sea.
drowned in the Red Sea.
drowned in the Red Sea.
drowned in the Red Sea. Doom,
61

63
- ry. Well, I'm sing - in', Ma -
Oh, Ma - ry, don't you weep.
Oh, Ma - ry, don't you weep.
Oh, Ma - ry, don't you weep.
Oh, Ma - ry, don't you weep.
doom, doom, doom, doom, doom, doom, doom, doom,
63
- ry. Well, I'm sing - in', Ma -
Oh, Ma - ry, don't you weep.
Oh, Ma - ry, don't you weep.
Oh, Ma - ry, don't you weep.
Oh, Ma - ry, don't you weep.
doom, doom, doom, doom, doom, bah, doom, doom, doom,
65

- ry. Think I need some - bod - y else to
Oh, Ma - ry, don't you weep.
Oh, Ma - ry, don't you weep.
Oh, Ma - ry, don't you weep.
Oh, Ma - ry, don't you weep.
doom, doom, doom, doom, doom, bah, doom, doom, doom,
67
help me. Call Ma - ry. Oh, oh,
Oh, Ma - ry, don't you weep. Oh, oh,
Oh, Ma - ry, don't you weep.
Oh, Ma - ry, don't you weep.
Oh, Ma - ry, don't you weep.
doom, doom, doom, doom, doom, doom, doom, doom,
69

71
oh, Ma - ry we're gon - na
oh, Ma - ry.
Oh, Ma - ry, don't you weep.
Oh, Ma - ry, don't you weep.
Oh, Ma - ry, don't you weep.
doom, doom, doom, doom, doom, doom, doom, doom, bah,
71
71
call her one more time. Oh, oh,
Oh, Ma - ry, don't you weep. Oh, oh,
Oh, Ma - ry, don't you weep. Oh, oh,
Oh, Ma - ry, don't you weep.
Oh, Ma - ry, don't you weep.
doom, doom, doom, doom, doom, doom, doom, doom,
73

75
oh, Ma - ry, Ma - ry, sing - in', Ma -
oh, Ma - ry, Ma - ry.
oh, Ma - ry, Ma - ry.
Oh, Ma - ry, don't you weep.
Oh, Ma - ry, don't you weep.
doom, doom, doom, doom, doom, doom, doom, doom,
75
75
- ry.
Some - bod - y needs ta tell it to
Oh, Ma - ry, don't you weep.
Oh, Ma - ry, don't you weep.
Oh, Ma - ry, don't you weep.
Oh, Ma - ry, don't you weep.
doom, doom, doom, doom, doom, doom, doom, doom,
77

79
Ma - ry. Oh, yeah, she don' have ta
Oh, Ma - ry, don't you weep.
Oh, Ma - ry, don't you weep.
Oh, Ma - ry, don't you weep.
Oh, Ma - ry, don't you weep.
doom, doom, doom, doom, doom, doom, doom, doom,
79
79
cry no more. You got - ta tell her you serve a
Oh, Ma - ry, don't you weep.
Oh, Ma - ry, don't you weep.
Oh, Ma - ry, don't you weep.
Oh, Ma - ry, don't you weep.
doom, doom, doom, doom, bah, doom, doom, doom, doom,
A♭maj9(no3♭5)/B♭
G♭(no5)/E♭7(no5)
81

83
might - y God. You don't have ta wor - ry 'bout your
Oh, Ma - ry, don't you weep.
Oh, Ma - ry, don't you weep.
Oh, Ma - ry, don't you weep.
Oh, Ma - ry, don't you weep.
doom, doom, doom, doom, doom, doom, doom, doom,
83
83
prob - lems. Don - cha, I know, I'm not
Oh, Ma - ry, don't weep.
Oh, Ma - ry, don't weep.
Oh, Ma - ry, don't weep.
Oh, Ma - ry, don't weep.
doom, doom, doom, doom, doom, doom, bah, doom, doom,
A♭9(no3,♭5)/E A♭maj9(no3,♭5)/E C4/A♭7(no3no5)
85

wor - ried 'bout to - mor - row; He'll bring joy for your sor - row. Don't you
Oh, Ma - ry, don't you weep.
Oh, Ma - ry, don't you weep.
Oh, Ma - ry, don't you weep.
Oh, Ma - ry, don't you weep.
doom, doom, doom, doom, doom, doom, doom, doom,
A♭9(no3♭5)/B♭
87
cry - y - y. No, no, oh, oh, oh,
Oh, Ma - ry, don't weep.
Oh, Ma - ry, don't weep.
Oh, Ma - ry, don't weep.
Oh, Ma - ry, don't weep.
doom, doom, doom, doom, doom, bah, do - om, bah, doom, bah, doom, bah,
G/A♭
B♭7(no5♯9)
89

91
oh. I know ya got
Oh, Ma - ry, don't you weep.
Oh, Ma - ry, don't you weep.
Oh, Ma - ry, don't you weep.
Oh, Ma - ry, don't you weep.
doom, doom, doom, doom, doom, doom, bah, doom, doom,
91
91
prob - lems, but don't weep 'cause Pha - roah's ar - my's been je -
Oh, Ma - ry, don't you weep.
Oh, Ma - ry, don't you weep.
Oh, Ma - ry, don't you weep.
Oh, Ma - ry, don't you weep.
doom, doom, doom, doom, doom, doom, doom, doom,
A♭9sus(no5)/E
93

rowned, je-rowned in the sea,
Pha - roah's ar - my
Pha - roah's ar - my
Pha - roah's ar - my
Pha - roah's ar - my
doom, Pha - roah's ar - my
95
yeah, Lawd. Sing - in', Ma - ry.
drowned in the Red Sea.
drowned in the Red Sea.
drowned in the Red Sea.
drowned in the Red Sea.
drowned in the Red Sea.
97

100 Slower (♩. = ca. 47)
Tell Mar-tha not
Oh, Ma - ry, don't you weep.
Oh, Ma - ry, don't you weep.
Oh, Ma - ry, don't you weep.
Oh, Ma - ry, don't you weep.
Oh, Ma - ry, don't you weep.
100 Slower (♩. = ca. 47)
99

to mourn.
Tell Mar - tha not to mo - (h)oan.
Tell Mar - tha not to mo - (h)oan.
Tell Mar - tha not to mo - (h)oan.
Tell Mar - tha not to mo - (h)oan.
Tell Mar - tha not to mo - (h)oan.
Cm(add4)/E♭
E♭(add2)
101

DAVID AND GOLIATH

For SATBBB a cappella

Duration: ca. 4:25

Arranged by
MARK KIBBLE

Traditional

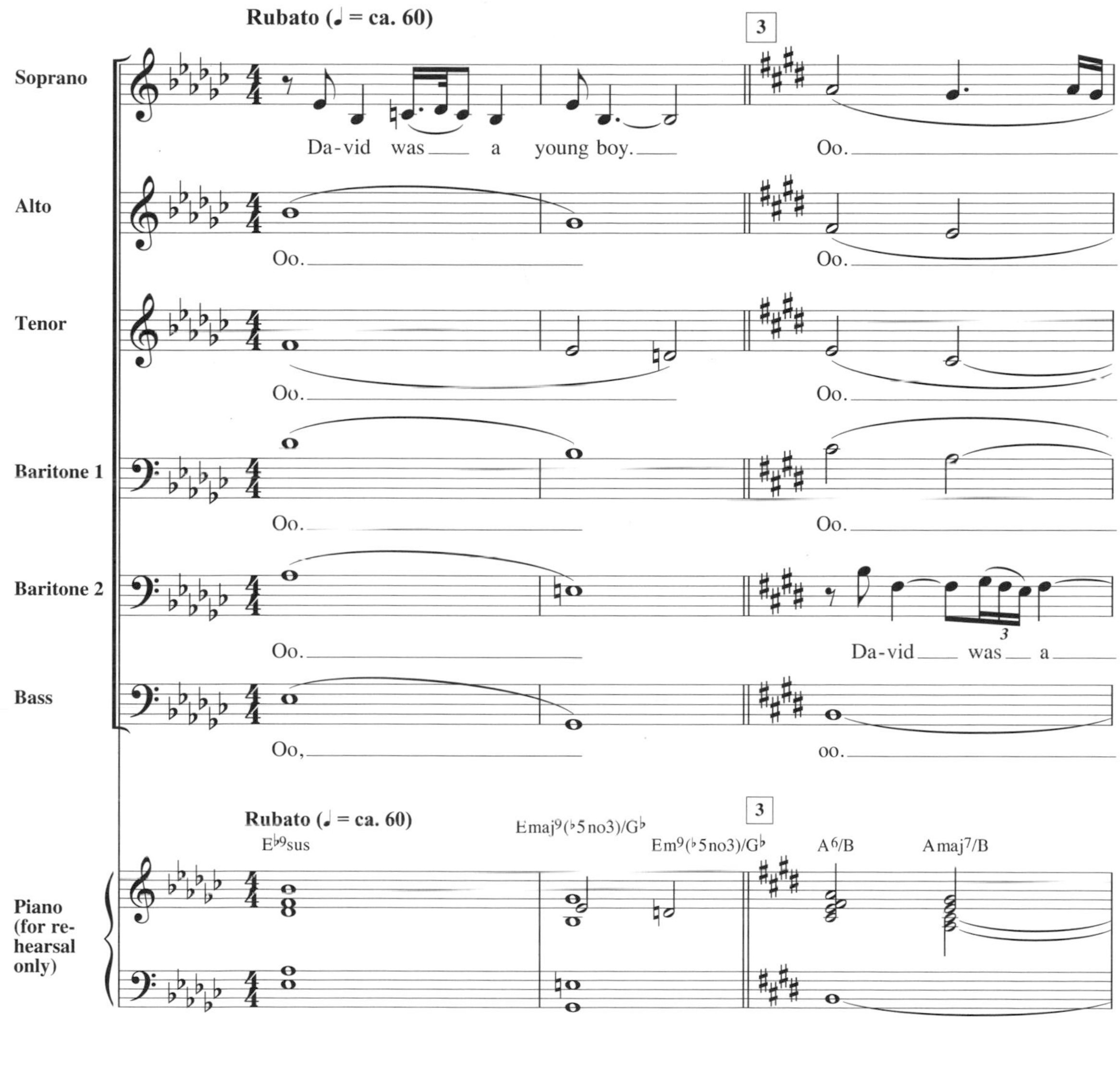

Visit Hal Leonard Online at
www.halleonard.com

5
But he looked like the jungle boy
looked like the jungle boy
looked like the jungle boy
looked like the jungle boy
strip-ling. looked like the jungle boy
looked like the jungle boy
B9
5
Fm11 Fm7 E♭m/G♭7(no5) E♭maj/G♭7(no5)
4
that was talked about by Kip-ling. Well, he
talked about by Oo. Well, he
talked about by Oo. Well, he
talked about by Oo. Well, he
talked about by Kip-ling. Well, he
talked about by Kip-ling. Well, he
A♭9sus/G♭ A♭m7(♭5)/B♭ Bdim7/B♭ A♭6(no3) E♭9sus E♭m(add2) E9sus(add6) F♯m9sus/A
7

10
looked like a jun - gle boy and he sang like a
looked like a jun - gle boy and he sang like a
looked like a jun - gle boy and he sang like a
looked like a jun - gle boy, oo.
looked like a jun - gle boy, oo.
looked like a jun - gle boy, oo.
F♯maj7/G♯ F♯maj9/G♯ F♯6/G♯ F♯maj7(♭5)/G♯ E♭m/E♭7(no5) E♭9sus/G♭ F♯maj9(no3)/G♯ G♭6/A♭
14
Swing behop feel (♩. = ca. 115)
bird.
bird.
bird.
Solo
3
But he fought like the dev - il when his tem - per got stirred. When
Bah-doom, doom, doo-min,
13

Bah, bah, bah, bah, oh.
Bah, bah, bah, bah, oh.
Bah, bah, bah, bah, oh.
Bah, bah, bah, bah, oh.
Da-vid was at-tend - ing sheep for his pa. Some-bod - y hol-lered. I
doom, bah-toom. Bah-toom, bah-toom. Bah-doom, doom, doom, doom,
A6 Bdim7 C♯m7 Fmaj7(♯5) Amaj9(no3) Gmaj9/A F♯ E♭(no5)
16
Whoa, bah, bah, bah, bah.
Whoa, bah, bah, bah, bah.
Whoa, bah, bah, bah, bah.
Whoa, bah, bah, bah, bah.
think it was his ma. She said, "Hur - ry to the field with this lit - tle bit-ty sack. I want you to
doom, doom, doom, doom, doom, bah-toom, bah-toom, bah-toom, bah-
F♯7sus/D Fmaj7(♭5)/G B2 G♯m(no 3) Fmaj9(♭5 no3)/C♯
19

22
oh, but hur - ry right back.
oh, but hur - ry right back.
oh, but hur - ry right back.
oh, but hur - ry right back.
take it to your broth-ers, but hur - ry right back." Now Da -
toom, doom, doom, but hur - ry right ba - ack. Bah -
22
Gmaj7(♭5)/A
F♯m7(♭5)/G♯
F♯11(♭5)/G♯
B4 / C♯(no5)
F♯m6/F♯
22
Doo, bah, doo, bah,
Doo, bah, doo, bah,
Doo, bah, doo, bah,
Doo, bah, doo, bah,
- vid took his lunch box and off he hur - ried. There
doom, doom, doom, doom, doom, doom, dum, bah - doom,
Gmaj9(♭5no3)/A
F♯m9(5♭no3)
24

doo, bah.
Oh,
doo, bah.
Oh,
doo, bah.
Oh,
doo, bah.
Oh,
he saw the Is-rael-ites look - in' right wor - ried. When he
doom, doom, doom, doom, doom, bah-doom, doom, doom,
F♯m(no 3)/E♭
F♯m7(no5add4)/D
26
30
oo. There he saw a sight
oo. There he saw a sight
oo. There he saw a sight
oo. There he saw a sight
asked them what the prob-lem was, they point-ed to the prair-ie. There he saw a sight
doom, doom, doom, doom, doom, doom, doom, doom. There he saw a sight
Bm7 F9(♯11no5) Em9 Gmaj7/D C♯m9
G♯m11 Daug/A♯7(no3no5) Bm9 Amaj/C♯7(no5)
28

to make an el - e-phant scar - y. Oh,
to make an el - e-phant scar - y. Oh,
to make an el - e-phant scar - y. Oh,
to make an el - e-phant scar - y. Oh,
to make an el - e-phant scar - y. Oh,
to make an el - e-phant scar - y. Oh,
G♯m7
Dmaj7(no3) / Fmaj7(♭5 no3)
31
there he saw Go - li - ath, cham - pi - on of Gath.
there he saw Go - li - ath, cham - pi - on of Gath.
there he saw Go - li - ath, cham - pi - on of Gath.
there he saw Go - li - ath, cham - pi - on of Gath.
there he saw Go - li - ath, cham - pi - on of Gath.
there he saw Go - li - ath, bah-doom, toom, toom, toom,
A13(♯11)
D2 / A♭7(no5)
D2 / C♯7(no5)
Fm11
F / E♭7(no5)
D9
Am9
D♭aug / E♭
34

38
He roared in his an - ger,
He roared in his an - ger,
He roared in his an - ger,
roared in his an - ger,
roared in his an - ger,
toom, doom, doom, doom, doom, doom, doom, doom, doom, doom, doom, doom,
38
Cmaj9(♭5)/D
Cmaj7(♯5)
37
howled in his wrath. Oh, he was strong - er than a li -
howled in his wrath. Oh, he was strong - er than a li -
howled in his wrath. Oh, he was strong - er than a li -
howled in his wrath. Oh, he was strong - er than a li -
howled in his wrath. Oh, he was strong - er than a li -
doom, doom, doom, doom, bahm doom, bah - doom, doom bah - doom, doom, doom, bah - doom,
Bm7(♭5)
Ddim7
40

- on. Oo, oo.
- on. Oo, oo.
- on. Oo, oo.
- on. Oo, oo.
- on; he was tall - er than a tree.
doom, do-pum-bah-doom, doom, doom, doom, doom, doom,
D9sus
A9sus(no5)
43
46
Lit - tle Da - vid had to
doom, doom, doom, bah-doom, bah - doom, do - oo - madoom, doom,
B4(add2)/D
A(add2)/D
A6/D
46
C6/D
45

reach up to his knee.
reach up to his knee.
reach up to his knee.
reach up to his knee.
tip - toe just to reach up to his knee.
doom, doom, doom, doom, reach up to his knee,
47
"Come out!" Doo, bah, bah, bah.
"Come out!" Doo, bah, bah, bah.
"Come out!" Doo, bah, bah, bah.
"Come out!" Doo, bah, bah, bah.
"Come out!" said the gi - ant, rag - ing and strid - ing.
so - oh low. "Come out!" Bah - doom, bah - doom, bah - doom, bah-
Fmaj7(♯5)
C♯7(no3,no5)
49

54
Oh, whoa. Bah, bah,
Oh, whoa. Bah, bah,
Oh, whoa. Bah, bah,
Oh, whoa. Bah, bah,
"Bring out your strong men from where ya got 'em hid-in'. Drag out your cham-pi-ons from
doom, doom, doom, doom, doom, doom, doom, doom, bah-doom, bah-doom, bah-
54
52
bah, bah, oo. oo,
bah, bah, oo. oo,
bah, bah, oo. oo,
bah, bah, oo. oo,
un-der the bunks. I'll feed 'em to the buz-zards, the liz-ards and the skunks." Now Da-
doom, bah-doom, bah-dah, doom, doom, doom, doom, doom, doom, doom. Bah-
F♯maj7(add2)/A♯ F♯6/B E9
55

doop, ah, doop, ah, doop. ah,
doop, ah, doop, ah, doop. ah,
doop, ah, doop, ah, doop. ah,
doop, ah, doop, ah, doop. ah,
- vid heard him brag - ging and said, "I de - clare. That gi - ant's got an aw - ful lot of
doom, doom, doom, doom, doom, doom, doom, bah - do - pum - bah - doom, doom, doom, doom,
58
62
oh, oo.
oh, oo.
oh, oo.
oh, oo.
Spoken:
mouth up there." So he strolled to the brook and he picked up a peb - ble; and it was
doom, bi - yoom, doom, doom, doom, doom, doom, doom, doom, doom, doom,
62
61

He starts out for the gi -
He starts out for the gi -
He starts out for the gi -
He starts out for the gi -
smooth as ice, but as hard as a dev-il. He starts out for the gi -
doom, doom, doom, doom, doom, doom, doom. He starts out for the gi -
Amaj7(♭5)/F
F♯9sus(no5)/D
64
- ant, dancing on his
- ant, dancing on his
- ant, dancing on his
- ant, dancing on his
- ant, dancing on his
- ant, ta - dan - ba-dee, dum, doom, bah -
67

70
toes. He was whirl - ing a-way with his sling -
toes. whirl - ing a-way with his sling -
toes. whirl - ing a-way with his sling -
toes. whirl - ing a-way with his sling -
toes. whirl - ing a-way with his sling -
doom, doom, ba, doom, doom, bah - doom, doom, doom, doom,
70
69
- shot. He was sing - ing a song like
- shot. He was sing - ing a song like
- shot. He was sing - ing a song like
- shot. He was sing - ing a song like
- shot. He was sing - ing a song like
doom, doom, doom, doom, doom, doom, doom, doom,
71

(♩ = ca. 76)
Clear throat
Classique highbrow style (♩ = ca. 110)
so, goes: "Rock of A - ges,
so goes: "Rock of A - ges,
Bmaj7/C♯
Bdim7/C♯
F♯
B/F♯
F♯/E
73
77
As before (♩. = ca. 115)
cleft for me." Like so.
Doom, doom, doom, doom, doom, doom, doom, doom, doom,

Doop, oo,
Doop, oo,
Doop, oo,
Doop, oo,
The giant looks at Da - vid and lets out a laugh. He
doom, doom, doom, doom, bah - doom, bah - doom, bah - doom, *(do, doom), doom,
A♭7sus(♭5)/E
D9(add6no5)
79
doop, oo.
Ha, ha, ha,
doop, oo.
Ha, ha, ha,
doop, oo.
Ha, ha, ha,
doop, oo.
Ha, ha, ha,
laughs a - like a tig - er be - ing sassed by a cat. He laughs like
doom, bah - doo, bop, be - ba - doom, bah - doom, doom,
82

*gruff laugh

84
ha. Doop, oo.
ha. Doop, oo.
ha. Doop, oo.
ha. Doop, oo.
a hy - e - na, grins from ear to ear. Ba - ba - ba -
doom, bah - doom, bah - doom, bah - doom, doom,
84
84
Dah, dah, dah, dah, dah, dah, dah, dah, dah, dah. He
Dah, dah, dah, dah, dah, dah, dah, dah, dah, dah. He
Dah, dah, dah, dah, dah, dah, dah, dah, dah, dah. He
Dah, dah, dah, dah, dah, dah, dah, dah, dah, dah. He
bang - in' on his ar - mor with his ten - foot spear.
do, do, bah-do, do. Dah, dah, dah, dah, dah, dah. He
E♭m7(♯5)/A♭
F♯(no5)
E♭7(no5)
86

starts out for Da - vid,
starts, starts out for Da - vid,
starts, starts out for Da - vid,
starts out for Da - vid,
starts out for Da - vid
starts, doom, doom, doom, doom, doom, bah-doom, doom,
F♯6
F♯m6
88
bang - in' and a - clank - in'.
bang - in' and a - clank - in'.
bang - in' and a - clank - in'.
bang - in' and a - clank - in'.
bang - in' and a - clank - in'.
Spoken:
bang - in' doom, doom, doom, doom, doom. He said,
90

92
Oo.
Oo.
Oo.
Oo.
Oo.
"Come here, jun - ior, (laughter) I'm a gon'
92
give you a span - kin'!"
Da - vid took his sling -
Da - vid took his sling -
Da - vid took his sling -
Da - vid took his sling -
Da - vid took his sling -
Bmaj7(no3add2)/D♯
95

- shot and he swung it 'round his head.
- shot and he swung it 'round his head.
- shot and he swung it 'round his head.
- shot and he swung it 'round his head.
- shot and he swung it 'round his head.
Doom, doom, doom, doom, doom, doom, doom, doom, doom,
Em7/D
97
100
Ou - oot f(a) - lew that peb - ble and the gi - ant
Ou - oot f(a) - lew that peb - ble and the gi - ant
Ou - oot f(a) - lew that peb - ble and the gi - ant
Ou - oot f(a) - lew that peb - ble and the gi - ant
Ou - oot f(a) - lew that peb - ble and the gi - ant
doom, doom, doom, doom, bah - doom, doom, doom, doom, doom, doom, doom, doom,
100
100

Boom!
dropped
dead!
dropped, he dropped dead! Bah-doom, bah - doom, doom, bah - doom. Ya
Fmaj7(♯5)/C♯7(no3,no5)
A♭4/G♭7(no5)
E9sus(no5)/C7(no3,no5)
A♭4/B7(no5)
Adim7/C
A♭4/D♭6♭9(no3)
103
Good shot!
know, lit-tle Da-vid made a good shot!
F♯13(♯11)
106

GET AWAY, JORDAN

For SATBBB a cappella

Duration: ca. 4:25

Arranged by
MARK KIBBLE

Traditional

Visit Hal Leonard Online at
www.halleonard.com

Get a - way, Jor - dan.
Oo
Oo
Oo
Oo
doom boom boom bah doom boom boom bah bah
F9sus
A♭maj7(♭5 add2)
5
doom boom boom bah doom boom boom bah
F♯9sus(no5add6)
C♯2/E
G♭9
B♭4(add2)/E
7

10
Get a - way, Jor - dan,
doom doom. Get a - way, Jor - dan, I want chu' to
E♭6
10 Fm7/A♭
9
get a - way, Jor - dan,
get a - way, get a - way, Jor - dan.
G♭maj9(♭5)/A♭
E♭m11 A♭9sus G♭maj9 A♭6sus/G♭ F♯6sus/A
11

get a - way,
Jor - dan, I
Get a - way, get a - way,
E♭6sus/A♭
Fm9 Fm7 A♭maj7(♭5)/B♭
13
wan - na cross o - va ta see my Law - d. Get a - way,
wan - na cross o - va ta see my Law - d. Get a - way,
D♭maj7/E♭ E♭9 G7(no5)
G♭6/E♭
G♭maj7(add2)
5

get a - way, Jor - dan,
get a - way, Jor - dan,
get a - way, Jor - dan,
get a - way, Jor - dan,
get a - way, Jor - dan,
doom doom. Get a - way, Jor - dan, I want you to
17
get a - way, Jor - dan,
get a - way, Jor - dan,
get a - way, Jor - dan,
get a - way, Jor - dan,
get a - way, Jor - dan,
get a - way, get a - way, Jor - dan,
19

get a - way, Jor - dan, I
get a - way, Jor - dan, I
get a - way, Jor - dan, I
get a - way, Jor - dan, I
get a - way, Jor - dan, I
get a - way, get a - way, Jor - dan, I
21
wan - na cross o - va ta see my Law - d.
wan - na cross o - va ta see my Law - d.
wan - na cross o - va ta see my Law - d.
wan - na cross o - va ta see my Law - d.
wan - na cross o - va ta see my Law - d.
wan - na cross o - va ta see my Law - d. You know that I
23

25
Bop oo, I
Bop oo, I
Bop oo, I
Bop oo, I
Bop oo, I
looked o - ver Jor - dan and what did I see? Bop, I
25
G♯m7/C D9 D♭9 Bmaj9(♭5) Emaj7/F♯ B♭m7(♯5add4)/B
25
wan - na cross o - va ta see my Law - d. Oo
wan - na cross o - va ta see my Law - d. Oo
wan - na cross o - va ta see my Law - d. Oo
wan - na cross o - va ta see my Law - d. Oo
wan - na cross o - va ta see my Law - d. Oo
wan - na cross o - va ta see my Law - d. I saw a
G♭6/A♭
27

29
bop oo, I
bop oo, I
bop oo, I
bop oo, I
bop oo, I
band of an - gels com - ing af - ter me. Bop, I
29
29
wan - na cross o - va ta see my Law - d. Get a - way,
wan - na cross o - va ta see my Law - d. Get a - way,
wan - na cross o - va ta see my Law - d. Get a - way,
wan - na cross o - va ta see my Law - d. Get a - way,
wan - na cross o - va ta see my Law - d. Get a - way,
wan - na cross o - va ta see my Law - d. Get a - way,
31

Measures 33 – 48 are optional

get a - way,
Jor - dan, I
get a - way, get a - way,
37
wan - na cross o - va ta see my Law - d.
wan - na cross o - va to see my Law - d. You know that I
39

41
Bop oo, I
Bop oo, I
Bop oo, I
Bop oo, I
Bop oo, I
went down to da riv - a, did - n't go fo' to stay. Bop, I
41
B maj9(♭5)/D♭
41
wan - na cross o - va ta see my Law - d. Oo
wan - na cross o - va ta see my Law - d. Oo
wan - na cross o - va ta see my Law - d. Oo
wan - na cross o - va ta see my Law - d. Oo
wan - na cross o - va ta see my Law - d. Oo
wan - na cross o - va ta see my Law - d. You know my
43

bop oo, I
bop oo, I
bop oo, I
bop oo, I
bop oo, I
soul got - a hap-py, stayed all day. Bop, I
45
wan - na cross o - va ta see my Law - d. Get a - way,
wan - na cross o - va ta see my Law - d. Get a - way,
wan - na cross o - va ta see my Law - d. Get a - way,
wan - na cross o - va ta see my Law - d. Get a - way,
wan - na cross o - va ta see my Law - d. Get a - way,
wan - na cross o - va ta see my Law - d. Get a - way,
47

get a - way, Jor - dan,
get a - way, Jor - dan,
get a - way, Jor - dan,
get a - way, Jor - dan, get a - way,
get a - way, Jor - dan, get a - way,
doom doom, get a - way, Jor - dan, get a - way,
F9sus/E♭ B♭m7(♭3)/F D13(♯11) E/D♭7(no5)
49
get a - way, oh, chil - ly Jor - dan get a - way,
get a - way, oh, chil - ly Jor - dan get a - way,
get a-way, oh, chil - ly Jor - dan get a - way,
oh, chil - ly Jor - dan get a - way,
oh, chil - ly Jor - dan get a - way,
a - way, oh, chil - ly Jor - dan get a - way,
E♭11(♭5)/F E♭11(♭5no3) G♯m/F7(no5) G♯m/D7(no5) B♭13(♯11) F♯m/A7(no5) G♭maj7(add6)/A♭
51

get a - way, Jor - dan, I wan - na cross
get a - way, Jor - dan, I wan - na cross
get a - way, Jor - dan, I wan - na cross,
get a - way, Jor - dan, oo, I
get a - way, Jor - dan, oo, I
get a - way, Jor - dan, oo, I
G♭7
A♭/F7(no5)
G4/B♭4
B♭sus/C B♭m7 F♯9(♭5no3)/A♭
A♭9(no5)
53
o - va ta see my Lawd. Get a - way,
o - va ta see my Lawd. Get a - way,
wan - na cross o - ver ta see my Lawd. Get a - way,
wan - na cross o - ver ta see my Lawd. Get a - way,
wan - na cross o - ver ta see my Lawd. Get a - way,
wan - na cross o - ver ta see my Lawd. Get a - way,
Csus/B♭7(no5)
A♭maj7(♯5)/B♭
A♭maj7/B♭
A♭2(add4)/G♭(no3)
55

get back, Jor - dan,
get back, Jor - dan,
8va
get back, Jor - dan,
8va
get back, Jor - dan,
8va
get back, Jor - dan,
doom bah doom doom bah doom hey hey hey, get a - way,
57
Spoken:
get a-way, oh, ch - ch - chil - ly Jor - dan, get a - way,
get a-way, oh, ch - ch - chil - ly Jor - dan, get a - way,
(8va)
get a-way, oh, ch - ch - chil - ly Jor - dan, get a - way,
(8va)
get a-way, oh, ch - ch - chil - ly Jor - dan, get a - way,
(8va)
get a-way, oh, ch - ch - chil - ly Jor - dan, get a - way,
get a-way, oh, ch - ch - chil - ly Jor - dan, get a - way,
Bm6/B♭7(no5)
Daug(add2)/B♭7(no5)
E♭9sus/G♭
Fm11
59

Legit choral style
get back, Jor - dan, oh, I
get back, Jor - dan, oh, I
get back, Jor - dan, oh, I
get back, Jor - dan, oh, I
get back, Jor - dan, oh, I
get back Jor - dan, oh, I
E♭9sus(no5)/B7(no5)
G4/B♭7(no5)
A♭maj6/B♭
Ddim7
A♭
61
wan - na cross o - va ta see my Lawd. Yes,
wan - na cross o - va ta see my Lawd. Yes,
wan - na cross o - va ta see my Lawd. Yes,
wan - na cross o - va ta see my Lawd. Yes,
wan - na cross o - va ta see my Lawd. Yes,
wan - na cross o - va ta see my Lawd. Doo doo doom. If re -
G♭dim7/E♭
E♭7
D♭9sus(no5)/E♭(no5)
63

65
bop oo, I
bop oo, I
bop oo, I
bop oo, I
bop oo, I
li - gion were a thing that cha mon - ey could buy, bop bop, I
65
65
wan - na cross o - va ta see my Law - d. Oo
wan - na cross o - va ta see my Law - d. Oo
wan - na cross o - va ta see my Law - d. Oo
wan - na cross o - va ta see my Law - d. Oo
wan - na cross o - va ta see my Law - d. Oo
wan - na cross o - va ta see my Law - d. You know that the
67

bop oo drop. I
bop oo drop. I
bop oo drop. I
bop oo drop. I
bop oo drop. I
Spoken:
rich would - a live and the poor would just drop. I
69
wan - na cross o - va ta see my Law - d. Get a - way,
wan - na cross o - va ta see my Law - d. Get a - way,
wan - na cross o - va ta see my Law - d. Get a - way,
wan - na cross o - va ta see my Law - d. Get a - way,
wan - na cross o - va ta see my Law - d. Get a - way,
wan - na cross o - va ta see my Law - d. Get a - way,
71

73
get back, Jor - dan,
get back, Jor - dan,
8va
get back, Jor - dan,
8va
get back, Jor - dan,
8va
get back, Jor - dan,
doom doom ba doom doo n doo n ba doom hey yay, get a -
73
73
Spoken:
get a - way, oh, ch - ch - chil - ly Jor - dan, get a - way,
get a - way, oh, ch - ch - chil - ly Jor - dan, get a - way,
(8va)
get a - way, oh, ch - ch - chil - ly Jor - dan, get a - way,
(8va)
get a - way, oh, ch - ch - chil - ly Jor - dan, get a - way,
(8va)
get a - way, oh, ch - ch - chil - ly Jor - dan, get a - way,
way - ee - ay, get a - way, oh, ch - ch - chil - ly Jor - dan, get a - way,
75

get back, Jor - dan, oh, I
get back, Jor - dan, oh, I
get back, Jor - dan, oh, I
get back, Jor - dan, oh, I
get back, Jor - dan, oh, I
get back, Jor - dan, oh, I
D♭7(no5)/E♭
77
79
building
wan - na cross the Jor - dan just ta see Him face to face, 'cause I be -
wan - na cross the Jor - dan just ta see Him face to face, 'cause I be -
wan - na cross the Jor - dan just ta see Him face to face, 'cause I be -
wan - na cross the Jor - dan just ta see Him face to face, 'cause I be -
wan - na cross the Jor - dan just ta see Him face to face, 'cause I be -
wan - na cross the Jor - dan just ta see Him face to face, 'cause I be -
79
Cmaj7(♭5 no3)/A♭
Bmaj7/D♭
Esus
G7(no5)
F♯m11
G/E
C♯4/E♭
building
79

rit. f
lieve He'll part the wa - ters if I have a lit - tle faith. So, get,
lieve He'll part the wa - ters if I have a lit - tle faith. So, get,
lieve He'll part the wa - ters if I have a lit - tle faith. So, get,
lieve He'll part the wa - ters if I have a lit - tle faith. So, get,
lieve He'll part the wa - ters if I have a lit - tle faith. So, get,
lieve He'll part the wa - ters if I have a lit - tle... Doo doo doo doo doo doo
E♭4/G♭7(no5)
E♭4/F
E♭sus/F
D♭maj9/E♭
81
get back, Jor - dan, got - ta get a -
get back, Jor - dan, got - ta get a -
get back, Jor - dan, got - ta get a -
get back, Jor - dan, got - ta get a -
get back, Jor - dan, got - ta get a -
doo doo doo doom doom doom ba doom doom ba
B4/A6(no5)
83

cross, get back, 'cause I wan - na see my Je - sus.
cross, get back, 'cause I wan - na see my Je - sus.
cross, get back, 'cause I wan - na see my Je - sus.
cross, get back, 'cause I wan - na see my Je - sus.
cross, get back, 'cause I wan - na see my Je - sus.
oom bah doom doo dom doom bah doom doom ah doom bah doom bah
B4 D7(no5)
Bm(add4)/A
A2 D7(no5)
85
No temp - ta - tion.
No temp - ta - tion.
No temp - ta - tion.
No temp - ta - tion.
No temp - ta - tion.
doom doom doom doom doom bah doom bah doom, is gon - na
A4 G7(no5)
87

Bop doo loo doo doo oo doo. So, I'm pray - in',
So, I'm pray - in',
So, I'm pray - in',
So, I'm pray - in',
So, I'm pray - in',
keep me from see - ing Him on the oth - er side. So, I'm pray - in',
Am11(♭5no3)/B
89
help me, Lord, and got - ta get a -
help me, Lord, and got - ta get a -
help me, Lord, and got - ta get a -
help me, Lord, and got - ta get a -
help me, Lord, and got - ta get a -
doom bop bah doom bah doom bah doom bah doom doot n dah doom bah
Bm7(♭3)/A(no3)
91

cross, split this Jor - dan,
cross, split this Jor - dan,
cross, split this Jor - dan,
cross, split this Jor - dan,
cross, split this Jor - dan,
doom doom doom doom doom doom bah doom doom
F♯m7
93
Legit choral style
Oo, get back, Jor - dan, oh, I
Oo, get back, Jor - dan, oh, I
Oo, get back, Jor - dan, oh, I
Oo, get back, Jor - dan, oh, I
Oo, get back, Jor - dan, oh, I
oo, get back, Jor - dan, oh, I
F♯m7
95

sfz
want to cross o - ver ta see my Lo - (h)ord. Yes, I
want to cross o - ver ta see my Lord. Doo doo doo doo doo doo. Yes,
97
wan - na cross o - ver ta see my Sav - ior face to face. I wan - na see
wan - na cross o - ver ta see my Sav - ior face to face. Yes, I
doom doom doom doom doom doom doom. Yes, I
G4
B7(no5)
E2
E7sus(no5) D(add2)/E E9sus
B♭maj7(♭5)/F♯
99

Je - sus,
ta see my Lawd.
sfz
got - ta get to the oth - er side.
Amaj7/B C♯m7/B
101
molto rit.
opt. trill
Jor - dan.
Get back,
Spoken:
Get back, get a-way, back, Jor - dan.
F7/G
A♭maj9(add6)
103

HE NEVER SLEEPS

For SATBBB a cappella

Duration: ca. 3:10

Arranged by
MARK KIBBLE

Traditional

Visit Hal Leonard Online at
www.halleonard.com

slum - bers. He watch - es me
slum - bers. He watch - es me
slum - bers. He watch - es me
slum - bers. He watch - es me
slum - bers. He watch - es me
slum - bers. He watch - es me
Dmaj9 C♯m7 A6/B G♯m7(add4)/E Cm7(♭5) B♭m7 Gm/E Daug/E
3
both night and day. He nev - er
both night and day and night. He nev - er
both night and day and night. He nev - er
both night and day and night. He nev - er
both day and night, night and day. He nev - er
both day and night. He nev - er
E♭9 D♭9sus(no5)/A7(no5) A7 D♭4/A7(no5) Bmaj7(add2)/A♭ B♭m9 E♭m11 D9(♯11) Bmaj9/C♯ Em/B♭7(no5)
6

9
sleeps; He never slumbers. The
sleeps; oo The
sleeps; oo The
sleeps; oo The
sleeps; He never slumbers. The
sleeps; oo The
9
E♭maj9 C4/E♭ E♭6 E♭m9(add4) G♭/E♭(no5) B♭m7/A♭ G♭6/A♭
9
reason I know– He told me
reason I know– He told me
reason I know– He told me
reason I know– He told me
reason I know– He told me
reason I know– He told me
A♭13(♯11) A♭9 G♭maj9(♭5)/A♭ G♯m9 G maj7(♭5)/E♭
12

15
Solo
so.
I don't have to wor - ry;
so.
oo
so.
oo
so.
oo
so.
oo
so.
oo
15
F♯m9/D
E9sus/G
Dmaj7/E
15
my soul's in His care.
I don'thave to
G9
Fmaj7/G
C♯m7/F♯
B♭maj7(♭5)/F♯
18

wor - ry; He'll al - ways be there.
oo
oo
oo
oo
oo
G9sus
Fmaj9(♭5 no3)/G
21
I know that He's watch - ing wher - ev - er I
oh woh oo woh
F♯m11(♭5)/G♯
Fmaj7(♯5)/G
24

end Solo
go.
I know that He's wa -
E/F♯4
Cm/F♯7(no5)
A/D
Bm7(♭5)/C♯
27
31
tching– He told me so. He nev - er
tching– He told me so. He nev - er
Amaj9/F♯
Bmaj9/A♭
E♭4/G♯m7(no5)
Bmaj9/D♭
Em9(♭5add6)/G
G♭sus/A♭
B♭aug(add2)/G♭7(no3no5)
30

slee - ps; He nev - er slum - bers.
slee - ps; slum - bers.
slee - ps; slum - bers.
slee - ps; slum - bers.
slee - ps; slum - bers.
slee - ps; slum - bers.
E♭9sus/G♭
33
He watch - es me both night and
He watch - es me both
He watch - es me both
He watch - es me both
He watch - es me both
He watch - es me both
A♭9sus(no5)
E7(no3no5)
36

41
day. He nev - er sleeps;
night and day. He nev - er sleeps;
night and day. He nev - er doo, doo,
night and day. He nev - er doo, doo,
night and day. He nev - er doo, doo,
night and day. Doo, doo,
D♭2
D♭(add 2)
G♯m7(no5)
Amaj7sus(add6)/B
Bm7
F♯9(no5)
39
He nev - er slum - bers. The rea-son I
He nev - er slum - bers.
doo, doo, doo, doo, doo, doo, doo,
doo, doo, doo, doo, doo, doo,
doo, doo, doo, doo, doo, doo,
doo, doo, doo, doo, doo, doo,
D/E
D♭maj9(♭5)/E♭
D13(♯11)
B♭7(♭5)/C
42

know– He told me
rea - son I know– He told me
rea - son I know– He told me
rea - son I know– He told me
rea - son I know– He told me
rea - son I know– He told me
F♯
B♭7(no5)
45
49
so. He nev - er sleeps; He nev - er
so. He nev - er sleeps; He nev - er
so. He nev - er sleeps; He nev - er
so. He nev - er sleeps; He nev - er
so. He nev - er sleeps; He nev - er
so. He nev - er sleeps; He nev - er
Gm
B♭7(no5)
Bm
B♭m7(no5)
G
B♭7(no5)
C9sus(no5)
E♭6(no5)
F4
E♭4
Fm7(no3)
E♭4
D♭aug7
49
48

slum - bers. He watch - es me
slum - bers. He watch - es me
slum - bers. He watch - es me
slum - bers. He watch - es me
slum - bers. He watch - es me
slum - bers. He watch - es me
C7sus / A♭(no5)
Fm7/A♭
E♭m / D♭4
D♭13(♭9♯11)
Ddim / E♭7(no5)
A♭7sus(no5) / E(no3)
51
both night and day. He nev - er
both night and day, day and night. He nev - er
both night and day, day and night. He nev - er
both night and day, day and night. He nev - er
both day and night, night and day. He nev - er
both day and night, night. He nev - er
54

57
sleeps; He nev - er slum - bers.
oo
oo
oo
oo
oo
rit.
57
Emaj9(♭5)/F♯
A6/B
Amaj7(add6)/F♯
57
A little faster (♩. = ca. 54)
The rea - son I know–
Amaj7(add6)/B
E♭m
A♭7(no5)
60

64
He told me so.
He told me so.
He told me so.
He told me so.
He told me so.
He told me so.
64
B/D♭9sus
F♯m/B6(no5)
64
Largo assai
He told me so.
He told me so.
He told me so.
He told me so.
He told me so.
He told me so.
Largo assai
Dmaj7(♭5)/E
B2/D2
E69(add5)/D
E9sus/G
E7sus/G
G♭(add2)
68

MILKY-WHITE WAY

For SATBBB a cappella

Duration: ca. 4:45

Arranged by
MARK KIBBLE

Words and Music by
MARK KIBBLE AND CLAUDE McKNIGHT

Visit Hal Leonard Online at
www.halleonard.com

way, child, one of these days.
oo, oo, one of these
oo, oo, one of these
oo, oo, one of these
oo, oo, one of these
oo, oo, one of these
B9(no5add6) F♯m6/B Dmaj7/E E7(add2) D7(add2)
3
Child, I'm go - ing to walk, walk that milk - y white
days. Oo,
days. Oo,
days. Oo,
days. Oo,
days. Oo,
Em7/A A7 D7sus(add2) D9sus D9(no5add6)
5

way, child, one of these days. Ah, well, well,
oo, oo, well, well, well,
oo, oo, well, well, well,
oo, oo, well, well, well,
oo, oo, well, well, well,
oo, oo, well, well, well,
F♯m7 B9 B13(no11) Dmaj9(no3♭5)
7
10
well, child, I'm gon - na walk on up and take my
we - (h)ll, oo, oo,
we - (h)ll, oo, oo,
we - (h)ll, oo, oo,
we - (h)ll, oo, oo,
we - (h)ll, oo, oo,
Dmaj7/E Dmaj7(♭5)/E
10
9

stand. Child, I'm gon - na join, join that Chris - tian
oo,
11
band. That's when - a we walk, walk that milk - y white
oo,
13

way, child, one of these days.
one of these days.
one of these days.
one of these days.
one of these days.
(solo)
one of these days. Child, I'm gon-na
15
18
Doo, doo, doo, doo, doo, doo, bah,
Doo, doo, doo, doo, doo, doo, bah,
Doo, doo, doo, doo, doo, doo, bah,
Doo, doo, doo, doo, doo, doo, bah,
Doo, doo, doo, doo, doo, doo, bah,
meet, meet my lov-ing moth-er, oh, child, one of these
18
G6(♭5)
Dmaj7(no3♭5♯9)
18

doo, bop, when I get there
doo, bop, when I get there
doo, bop, when I get there
doo, bop, when I get there
doo, bop, when I get there
days. Oh, yeah, don't you know. Child, I'm gon - na
Gmaj9(♭5)
Gmaj7
Gmaj9
D♭7(no5)/G
20
dah, dat, dat, shah, dah, dat, dah, dah, oo,
dah, dat, dat, shah, dah, dat, dah, dah, oo,
dah, dat, dat, shah, dah, dat, dah, dah, oo,
dah, dat, dat, shah, dah, dat, dah, dah, oo,
dah, dat, dat, shah, dah, dat, dah, dah, oo,
meet, meet my lov - ing moth - er, oh, one of these
F♯m7(♭5)
A6
F2
Adim(no3)
22

well, well, well, well, yeah, yeah.
well, well, well, well, yeah, yeah,
days, a - well, well, a - I, I'm go - ing to
D4(add2)/G♯
D9sus(no5)/G
24
26
Oo, oo, oo,
walk on up and take her hand when we reach when we reach that
Cmaj7(no3 add2)/G♯
G6sus(add2)

oo, ah, oo, ah,
oo, ah, ah, oo, ah,
oo, ah, ah, oo, ah,
oo, ah, ah, oo, ah,
oo, ah, ah, oo, ah,
prom - iscd land when we walk, walk that milk - y white
B♭maj7(♯5)/E
29
oo, oo. One of these…
oo, oo, one of these
oo, oo, one of these
oo, oo, one of these
oo, oo, one of these
way. Oh, child, one of these days.
F♯m7(♭5)
31

34
Child, I'm gon-na meet, oh, meet God the
days. Goin' to meet, goin' to meet,
days. Goin' to meet, goin' to meet,
days. Goin' to meet, goin' to meet,
days. Goin' to meet, goin' to meet,
Bom, bom, bom, bom, bom, bom, bom, goin' to meet, goin' to meet,
34
33
Fa - ther, and God the Son.
goin' to meet, goin' to meet, goin' to meet God and the
goin' to meet, goin' to meet, goin' to meet God and the
goin' to meet, goin' to meet, goin' to meet God and the
goin' to meet, goin' to meet, goin' to meet God and the
goin' to meet, goin' to meet, goin' to meet God and the
D9
35

Gon - na meet God the
Son. Goin' to meet, goin' to meet,
Son. Goin' to meet, goin' to meet,
Son. Goin' to meet, goin' to meet,
Son. Goin' to meet, goin' to meet,
Son. Goin' to meet, goin' to meet,
37
Fa - ther and God the Son, well, God the
goin' to meet, goin' to meet, goin' to meet, goin' to meet,
goin' to meet, goin' to meet, goin' to meet, goin' to meet,
goin' to meet, goin' to meet, goin' to meet, goin' to meet,
goin' to meet, goin' to meet, goin' to meet, goin' to meet,
goin' to meet, goin' to meet, goin' to meet, goin' to meet,
E7
B(add 2)
39

42
Son. Whoa, goin' to meet, hey, hey,
goin' to meet, goin' to meet, goin' to meet, goin' to, oh,
goin' to meet, goin' to meet, goin' to meet, goin' to, oh,
goin' to meet, goin' to meet, goin' to meet, goin' to, oh,
goin' to meet, goin' to meet, goin' to meet, goin' to, oh,
goin' to meet, I am goin' to meet, I am goin' to mett, goin' to, oh,
42
41
yeah. I'm gon-na meet God the
goin' to meet, goin' to meet, goin' to meet, goin' to meet,
goin' to meet, goin' to meet, goin' to meet, goin' to meet,
goin' to meet, goin' to meet, goin' to meet, goin' to meet,
goin' to meet, goin' to meet, goin' to meet, goin' to meet,
goin' to meet, goin' to meet, goin' to meet, goin' to meet,
Gmaj7(♯5)/A
43

Fa - ther and Son. Well, I'm gon - na meet, meet God the
goin' to meet, goin' to meet, goin' to, oh, goin' to meet,
goin' to meet, goin' to meet, goin' to, oh, goin' to meet,
goin' to meet, goin' to meet, goin' to, oh, goin' to meet,
goin' to meet, goin' to meet, goin' to, oh, goin' to meet,
goin' to meet, goin' to meet, goin' to, oh, goin' to meet,
B♭maj7(♭5)/F♯
45
Fa - ther and God the Son.
goin' to meet, goin' to meet, goin' to meet God and the
goin' to meet, goin' to meet, goin' to meet God and the
goin' to meet, goin' to meet, goin' to meet God and the
goin' to meet, goin' to meet, goin' to meet God and the
goin' to meet, goin' to meet, goin' to meet God and the
47

50
There's noth - in' that I want more, oh, oo, oh, oo,
Son. Goin' to meet, goin' to meet,
Son. Goin' to meet, goin' to meet,
Son. Goin' to meet, goin' to meet,
Son. Goin' to meet, goin' to meet,
Son. Goin' to meet, goin' to meet,
50
49
than to see the Fa-ther and God the
goin' to meet, goin' to meet, goin' to meet, goin' to meet,
goin' to meet, goin' to meet, goin' to meet, goin' to meet,
goin' to meet, goin' to meet, goin' to meet, goin' to meet,
goin' to meet, goin' to meet, goin' to meet, goin' to meet,
goin' to meet, goin' to meet, goin' to meet, goin' to meet,
51

Son. When I get to heav-en, I'm gon-na see;
goin' to meet, goin' to meet, goin' to meet, goin' to, oh,
goin' to meet, goin' to meet, goin' to meet, goin' to, oh,
goin' to meet, goin' to meet, goin' to meet, goin' to, oh,
goin' to meet, goin' to meet, goin' to meet, goin' to, oh,
goin' to meet, I am goin' to meet, I am goin' to meet, goin' to, oh,
53
I see my might-y God and the Son, who
goin' to meet, goin' to meet, goin' to meet, goin' to meet,
goin' to meet, goin' to meet, goin' to meet, goin' to meet,
goin' to meet, goin' to meet, goin' to meet, goin' to meet,
goin' to meet, goin' to meet, goin' to meet, goin' to meet,
goin' to meet, goin' to meet, goin' to meet, goin' to meet,
55

58
died for me. When I get to heav - en, gon - na see
goin' to meet, goin' to meet, goin' to, oh, goin' to meet,
goin' to meet, goin' to meet, goin' to, oh, goin' to meet,
goin' to meet, goin' to meet, goin' to, oh, goin' to meet,
goin' to meet, goin' to meet, goin' to, oh, goin' to meet,
goin' to meet, goin' to meet, goin' to, oh, goin' to meet,
58
57
the Fa - ther and the Son.
goin' to meet, goin' to meet, goin' to meet God and the
goin' to meet, goin' to meet, goin' to meet God and the
goin' to meet, goin' to meet, goin' to meet God and the
goin' to meet, goin' to meet, goin' to meet God and the
goin' to meet, goin' to meet, goin' to meet God and the
59

62
Goin' to see the Father, meet with the
Son. Goin' to see the Father, meet with the
Son. Goin' to see the Father, meet with the
Son. Goin' to see the Father, meet with the
Son. Goin' to see the Father, meet with the
Son. Goin' to see the Father. Bom, bom, bom, bom,
G♭maj9(♭5)/G♯
62
Fmaj9
61
Father. Don't you wanna see the Father, oh, oh, oh, see the
Father. Don't you wanna see the Father, oh, oh, oh, see the
Father. Don't you wanna see the Father, oh, oh, oh, see the
Father. Don't you wanna see the Father, see the
Father. Don't you wanna see the Father, see the
spoken:
Father. Don't you wanna see the Father, sa - sa - see the
B♭maj9/C
F♯m7(♭5)/E
D/E
63

66
Fa - ther and see Je - sus, and see my
Fa - ther and see Je - sus, dum, dum, da, and see my
E♭13(♯11)
66 D13(no11)
Am9 Am11 Am7
65
Je - sus when we walk that milk - y white way - ay - ay? But I'm
Je - sus when we walk that milk - y white way - ay - ay - ay?
Je - sus when we walk that milk - y white way - ay?
Je - sus when we walk that milk - y white way?
67

70
go - in some day. I'm gon - na
Goin' to meet, goin' to, oh, goin' to meet, goin' to meet,
Goin' to meet, goin' to, oh, goin' to meet, goin' to meet,
Goin' to meet, goin' to, oh, goin' to meet, goin' to meet,
Goin' to meet, goin' to, oh, goin' to meet, goin' to meet,
Goin' to meet, I am goin' to, oh, goin' to meet, I am goin' to meet,
70
70
walk that milk - y white way.
goin' to meet, goin' to meet, goin' to meet, goin' to meet,
goin' to meet, goin' to meet, goin' to meet, goin' to meet,
goin' to meet, goin' to meet, goin' to meet, goin' to meet,
goin' to meet, goin' to meet, goin' to meet, goin' to meet,
goin' to meet, I am goin' to meet, goin' to, I am goin' to meet,
72

74
Gon - na see the Fa - ther and God
goin' to, oh, goin' to meet, goin' to meet, goin' to meet,
goin' to, oh, goin' to meet, goin' to meet, goin' to meet,
goin' to, oh, goin' to meet, goin' to meet, goin' to meet,
goin' to, oh, goin' to meet, goin' to meet, goin' to meet,
goin' to, oh, goin' to meet, goin' to meet, goin' to meet,
74
74
wah, ah, ah, ah, the Son. Doo, doo, doo, doo, doo,
goin' to meet God and the Son. Goin' to see the
goin' to meet God and the Son. Goin' to see the
goin' to meet God and the Son. Goin' to see the
goin' to meet God and the Son. Goin' to see the
goin' to meet God and the Son. Goin' to see the
76

78
doo, doo, I do why don't why - hy.
Fa - ther; meet with the Fa - ther. Don't you wan - na see the
Fa - ther; meet with the Fa - ther. Don't you wan - na see the
Fa - ther; meet with the Fa - ther. Don't you wan - na see the
Fa - ther; meet with the Fa - ther. Don't you wan - na see the
Fa, dum, da-oom, du-boom, ba, doom, the Fa - ther. Do - on't you wan - na see the
78
Don't you wan-na see Him?
Fa - ther, oh, oh, oh, see the Fa - ther and see
Fa - ther, oh, oh, oh, see the Fa - ther and see
Fa - ther, oh, oh, oh, see the Fa - ther and see
Fa - ther, see the Fa - ther and see
Fa - ther, doom, doom, ba, doom, the Fa - ther and see
80

82
Yeah - eh - eh.
Je - sus,
Je - sus, and see my Je - sus when we
Je - sus, and see my Je - sus when we
Je - sus, and see my Je - sus when we
Je - sus, and see my Je - sus when we
Je - sus, doom, doo, and see my Je - sus when we
82
D9(♯11no5)
82
wah,
walk that milk - y white way - ay - ay - ay?
walk that milk - y white way - ay - ay?
walk that milk - y white way - ay?
walk that milk - y white way?
walk that doom, doom, milk - y white way?
84

86
woo, oo, I'm gon - na
Goin' to meet, goin' to, oh goin' to meet, goin' to meet,
Goin' to meet, goin' to, oh goin' to meet, goin' to meet,
Goin' to meet, goin' to, oh goin' to meet, goin' to meet,
Goin' to meet, goin' to, oh goin' to meet, goin' to meet,
Goin' to meet, goin' to, oh, goin' to meet, I am goin' to meet,
86
A13(♯11no9)
86
meet, God the Fa - ther and Son. Well, I'm gon - na
goin' to meet, goin' to meet, goin' to meet, goin' to meet,
goin' to meet, goin' to meet, goin' to meet, goin' to meet,
goin' to meet, goin' to meet, goin' to meet, goin' to meet,
goin' to meet, goin' to meet, goin' to meet, goin' to meet,
goin' to meet, I am goin' to meet, goin' to meet, I am goin' to meet,
88

meet, meet God the Fa - ther. Don't you wan - na see
goin' to, oh, goin' to meet, goin' to meet, goin' to meet,
goin' to, oh, goin' to meet, goin' to meet, goin' to meet,
goin' to, oh, goin' to meet, goin' to meet, goin' to meet,
goin' to, oh, goin' to meet, goin' to meet, goin' to meet,
goin' to, oh, goin' to meet, goin' to meet, goin' to meet,
90
92
Je - sus? Won't you come and walk with me when we
goin' to, oh, goin' to meet, goin' to meet, goin' to meet,
goin' to, oh, goin' to meet, goin' to meet, goin' to meet,
goin' to, oh, goin' to meet, goin' to meet, goin' to meet,
goin' to, oh, goin' to meet, goin' to meet, goin' to meet,
goin' to, oh, goin' to meet, goin' to meet, goin' to meet,
92
92

meet the Fa - ther, oh, and the
goin' to, oh, goin' to meet, goin' to meet, goin' to meet,
94
rit.
Son? God and the, uh, Son.
goin' to meet God and the, uh, Son.
96

LET THE WORDS

For SATBBB a cappella

Duration: ca. 1:00

Arranged by
MERVYN WARREN

Words and Music by
GAIL HAMILTON

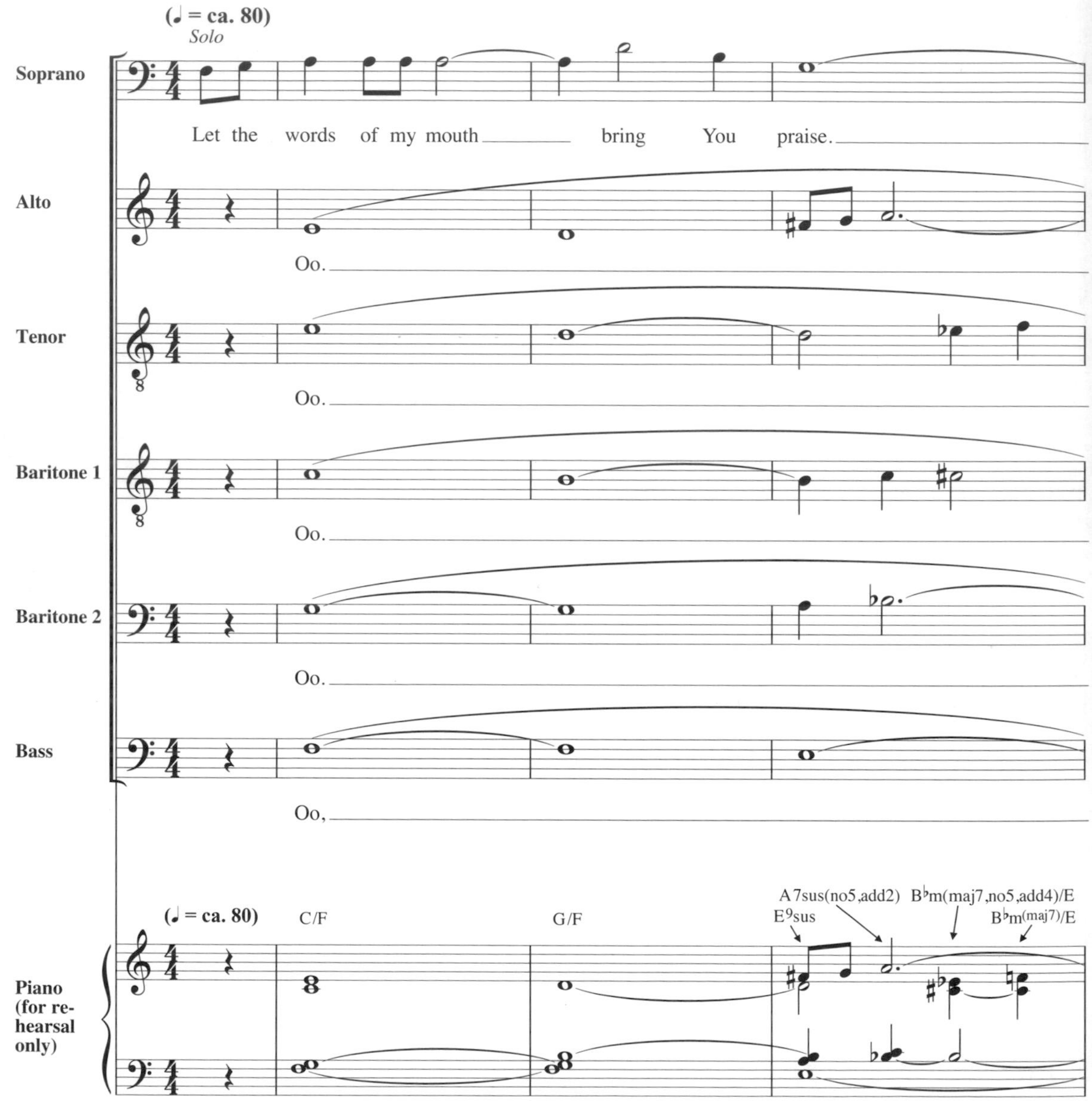

Let the words that I speak be sea - soned with Your love and
Oo.
oo.
B♭maj7(♯5)/E Gm/E Gm11(b5no3)/A
G4/A
Gsus/A♭
Fmaj7(no5)/G
4
grace.
May the things, O Lord, that I choose to say bring
Oo,
E7sus/G Am/G Em9(♯5)/G C/G
B♭maj7/C
B♭/C
Fmaj9
D/E
Fdim7/E
7

glo - ry, not shame, to Your name each day. Let the words of my mouth
Cmaj7(no5)/A Fmaj7/A Am7 C/Dsus D9 Dm11
11
bring You praise.
bring You, let them bring You praise.
bring You, let them bring You praise.
bring You praise, ah.
bring You, let them bring You... ah.
bring You, let them bring You... ah.
Am/B♭ C6(add2)/B♭ B♭maj9 Em/G7(no5) E/G7(no5) A♭maj9 A♭(add2)/G♭ D7(♭5 ♭9) C
14